To Gordon

Love and Best

"Great Memories"

Jarrett !!

The Best 80 Years

The Best 80 Years

Tony Best

YouCaxton Publications
Oxford & Shrewsbury

ISBN 978-191117-505-6

Printed and bound in Great Britain.

Published by YouCaxton Publications 2016

FOREWORD

by Raymond Froggatt

I met Tony Best a long time ago. He was then a troubadour of song and comedy entertainment, "A One Man Show." His performances reached the hearts of everyone in the audiences of his days on stage.

Tony Best became far more than that. He created a family of people he didn't know. Still today, this family of people sit around the warm fire of laughter and entertainment, and in their joy of thinking, remember all things good.

Tony Best pioneered the long weekend, and sometimes longer periods of holiday breaks and country music holidays. Tony did this without the benefit of social media and freeview showcase TV stations.

He created "the club magazine" in which he featured his up and coming events and he showcased his stars of entertainment. Tony Best was, and still is, at the forefront of every show he promotes, with a full input of personal entertainment, with his natural comic and warm talents as genial host.

In these pages, there is a story of an entertainment man who achieved extraordinary things in an extraordinary business. These extraordinary things are now emulated by many other people, and I think he can be very proud of that.

When the moments of joy and friendships become golden memories, the rainbow and fine sunshine of great days will remain like stars, and at the top of that rainbow will be the name, Tony Best, shining down on the family he created and loves still.

"Read on."

Raymond Froggatt

CONTENTS

INTRODUCTION

It is July 2015 and I am now officially retired – a gentleman of leisure. With supposedly plenty of time to do all those things which have been put off for years. Approaching the age of eighty I have come to the end of my working life; celebrating this milestone with a wonderful weekend in Blackpool with family and friends and over four hundred guests. Just how did this happen?

I was born and brought up in the Vale of Glamorgan, South Wales. After my childhood there my life seemed to go in stages; all quite different to each other in content and like living totally different lives. For instance; from the age of seventeen I was in the Royal Air Force for fifteen years; followed by a sort of in between life for nearly eight years on the Isle of Anglesey in beautiful North Wales. During this time I spent periods as a steward of a social club, licensee of a public house, proprietor of a music shop, a singer in the local pubs and clubs, an entertainment agent and promoter, and as a singer and musician in a popular semi-professional club band.

This led to my life on the road for fifteen years as a professional musician and entertainer; during which time I travelled all over the country and to several places abroad on short trips as a visiting artiste. It was during this time that I got into something which was to be my interest as well as my business for years to come; country music. And so I started up the Lazyacre Country Music Club in Shrewsbury; which is still going strong to this day and has been a very enjoyable hobby for the last thirty-eight years.

My time as a travelling entertainer also led to the next stage; in the mid 1980s my wife Jean and I had the opportunity to form our own holiday company which we called Tony Best Leisure. Our business was to book hotels and holiday centres; to organise and present country music holidays around Britain, mostly on the coast. This was an exciting period in our lives which takes us right up to the present day.

So my life has been a series of separate sections, each one completely different to the previous one, and each one most enjoyable in its own way. I have always spent my time playing music and entertaining; even whilst in the RAF. Whilst running Tony Best Leisure I continued to tour the country with my own shows; so the stages have overlapped but have felt very separate and distinct.

In the very early days of Tony Best Leisure the business was something of a one man operation; with me doing everything from booking the venues, engaging and contracting the artistes, right up to running the events when they took place. When TBL had been running for ten years I asked our daughter Lynne to work full time for the company to help me cope with the ever-increasing workload of the growing business.

Another ten years went by and Jean and I decided that it was time to take things easier; I went into semi-retirement by handing the business on to Lynne for her to run; with me staying in the background to offer help and advice when Lynne thought it was needed.

Another ten years flew past and at the age of seventy-nine I decided it really was time for me to retire properly. This was the time that Lynne came to the conclusion that she really did not want to run the business on her own; without the help and company of Jean and me so together and so we took the decision to close down Tony Best Leisure in July 2015. It was a difficult decision to make, but I am sure it was the right one.

2015 was exactly thirty years from when we formed Tony Best Leisure and we decided to present some special celebration events in the spring and summer of that year to mark the company's 30th anniversary. This culminated in our very special final weekend in July in Blackpool; arranged to take place exactly thirty years to the day from our first event there in 1985. The great success of these events at Bracklesham Bay in Sussex, Gunton Hall in Suffolk and finally at the Norbreck Castle Hotel in Blackpool meant that we really went out on a high.

I am writing this page just three days after TBL's final event in Blackpool; where over four hundred guests together with our team of resident and visiting entertainers all participated in what turned out to be a tremendously enjoyable though very emotional final fling.

At this final weekend several of our guests asked me, 'What are you going to do with all the spare time that you will have after you've retired?' Each time I answered them in the same way with 'Well I've got a book to write for a start!'

Over the years speaking to people and recalling some amusing and enjoyable experiences of my years on tour or at our events many have said, 'You should write a book!' So I promised myself that I would do exactly that one day – and now that day has arrived. I sit here in my little office at home in Shrewsbury with a blank sheet of paper in front of me thinking to myself, 'Where do I start?' and, 'what could I write about which would be of any interest to anyone other than my immediate family?' Fortunately I have been blessed with a good memory; and I have a great many anecdotes and stories that I have always loved to share.

I have led a totally unplanned life. Apart from the decision I made at school that I was going to join the RAF. Things simply happened which led me to move on; and often to move on in a most unexpected direction. I think they call it going with the flow. Let me tell you about it.

Pass me that blank sheet of paper and I'll get cracking.

CHAPTER 1

My Early Days

I was christened Anthony and I spent the first forty years of my life known as Tony Jarrett, my real name. So anyone who knew me from childhood right through to forty years of age will know me by that name. From then on I settled on a stage name; my family and I moved to Shrewsbury and everybody came to know me as Tony Best. Only government departments like HMRC or my family still use Jarrett. So I have had forty years as Tony Jarrett and about forty years as Tony Best, although during my RAF years I was Taff Jarrett. But enough about this; let us start at the very beginning.

I came into this world on the 4th of March 1936 in the little coastal village of East Aberthaw in the Vale of Glamorgan, South Wales. My brother Peter was thirteen when I was born and my sister, Peggy was nine. Dad, who was an analytical chemist at the Aberthaw Cement Works, was fifty. My Mum was forty so obviously I was a mistake! You wouldn't have known it though; my brother and sister always said that I was spoilt rotten and that I got away with far more than they ever had. Mum and Dad did not care for the term mistake; they preferred to call me an afterthought!

My Dad Ken hailed from Gillingham, one of the Medway towns in Kent. He was a *Man of Kent*, because he was born east of the River Medway; if he had been born west of the river he would have been a *Kentish Man*! My Mum Annie was Welsh and came from Llangranog, a little seaside village on Cardigan Bay in West Wales. She was very proud of her Welsh heritage and very proud to be a *Cardy*. Mum and Dad came together in the Vale of Glamorgan through their work at Aberthaw. My Mum did clerical work at the cement works for a while; she left after marrying my Dad to become what these days is known as a full time Mum.

A central feature of the village of East Aberthaw was the huge superbly thatched 14th century pub, The Blue Anchor. Established in 1380 it was one of the oldest pubs in Wales. Apart from a forced closure in 2004 (due to a serious fire which destroyed the thatched roof,; now restored) The Blue Anchor Inn has traded continuously as a public house since 1380. This famous pub has been owned by the same family, the Colemans, since 1941. At that time the inn was a focal point for the thriving trading port of Aberthaw; which in those days was a more important port than those nearby at Cardiff, Penarth and Barry. The port of Aberthaw was synonymous with smuggling; and was busy enough to justify a Customs & Excise presence. I remember how as children when we were playing in the village we would knock on the side window of the pub to be served with pop and crisps. When we sang carols at Christmas we would be invited into the bar of the pub to sing our carols for the locals. This was something which felt like an adventure; and which we children always looked forward to.

Ours was a musical family. Mum and Dad both played the piano. Mum played the organ in the village church; I was in the choir – complete with cassock and surplice! My brother Peter played piano accordion and my sister Peg played piano and accordion in a local dance band. Peter was in the Fleet Air Arm during the war so there was just Peggy and me at home with Mum and Dad. I would constantly pester Peg to come into the front room (the parlour) to play a tune on the piano and I would sing along to all the hits of the day from the piles of sheet music she had. We lost my sister a few years back. Just a few weeks ago Jean, Lynne and I visited our niece Jacqueline (Peg's daughter) in Barry; she said to me, 'I've got something for you.' She left the room and returned with a case full of all that sheet music from the old house in Aberthaw. I could not believe it; I was so thrilled. It took me right back to those sessions in the parlour.

The village of East Aberthaw was very tiny, just 166 people including half a dozen kids about the same age as me and we were all great pals. I know it was 166 people at the time because when I was about seven I took it into my head to do a census of the village; and that was the exact number of inhabitants. I presented my census as a project when I next went to Cubs and got commended for it. I was so proud!

East Aberthaw was a great little village to grow up in. I delivered newspapers every morning and had another paper round in the evenings delivering the *South Wales Echo* and so I knew everyone in the village by name. My favourite was Mrs Hoye who kept the post office and newsagents; she was the lady I delivered the papers for. I think I must have been her blue-eyed boy because she used to give me her sweet coupons!

We lived in a house called The Laurels at one end of the village. It was one of a semi-detached pair of houses – the other one was Sea View; they were owned by the cement works where my Dad worked. I loved The Laurels; it had a small lawn at the front of the house and at the side was a big garden where Dad grew all the vegetables. There was another long garden at the back of the house for more vegetables and fruit bushes with black and redcurrants, gooseberries and raspberry canes. The path up the middle of the garden took us up to the outhouse, known as the lav.

Though The Laurels sounds quite posh it was in fact a bit primitive as there was no flush toilet, just an outhouse twenty yards up the path at the end of the garden. I was about twelve years old when the cement company built us a little extension on the back of the house, containing a flush toilet. We had really come up in the world; no more would the man come to our house every Tuesday. His lorry had a huge container on the back. Into this he would empty the waste from the bucket he had extracted from our loo; carried down the garden path around the side of the house to be emptied into this container. What a job! Our 'lavatory man' as we called him was Mr Ball, who was actually our coalman. The rest of the week he delivered coal but for one day a week this was his sideline. So we were not really posh and neither was anyone else in the village.

However we were one of only about six houses in the village which had a bathroom. This was upstairs and the bath had one tap – cold of course. In our back kitchen we had a big copper, a boiler which could hold about eight buckets of water, and it had a coal fire underneath to heat the water. So on bath night Mum would light the fire; and when the water was boiling it had to be carried in buckets upstairs to the bathroom.

I do not ever remember Mum lighting this fire in a conventional way, with sticks and paper and then a bit of coal. She would just go through into the living room with a big shovel and carry a shovelful of 'fire' into the back kitchen and deposit it under the copper. Straight away there was a fire in both rooms. No one had heard of health and safety then! She used the same system when we were going to use the front room (the parlour – that sounds posh too!) She would carry the shovelful of fire down the passageway and into the front room, and the job was done.

I mention that there were only about six houses in the village which could boast a bathroom as during the war there was an army searchlight battalion based a couple of miles outside Aberthaw. The troops manning this place needed a bath once a week and arrangements were made for them to have their baths in one of the houses. So once a week about half a dozen squaddies would turn up at our house, have their baths, come down afterwards and have a cup of tea before going back to camp. They even carried the buckets of hot water upstairs themselves. I think Mum got a few shillings each week for providing this service.

Over the wall at the end of the back garden path was a field where the local farmer used to graze his cattle and where we used to play. The side wall of ours and next door's outhouses was just the right size for a chalk drawn goal when we used to play football.

Our school was two miles away in the next village – Rhoose. It was two miles on the bus going to school because we were the last pick up; going home was different. We were the last drop off on the way home so it was about fifteen miles journey around seven villages in the Vale of Glamorgan. I was very happy at that school, mainly because of the large sports field and the main hall where on the nearest school day to March 1st (St David's Day) they held an Eisteddfod at which I always sang. I would either sing a traditional Welsh song *Aderyn Pur* (in the Welsh language) or the Stephen Adams classic *The Holy City*. I was always very nervous of singing in front of the whole school (parents, teachers and children) but I would go on stage and whilst I was singing I would fix my gaze on the clock high on the back wall of the hall. The image of that wall clock is imprinted on my memory; but it got me through my nerves.

I do not remember much about the winters of those times apart from the amazing winter of 1947 when we had toboggans and it was so frozen up that we could skate on the river. I do remember the summers though because every summer was a joy. The summers seemed to be much longer then and until school broke up for the holidays we would rush to get home from school. We would quickly change then it was straight across the road, over the railway bridge, through the railings on the other side, slide down the embankment and we were on the beach where we could swim until it got dark. In the school holidays we were down there from morning until teatime. They were great days.

Away from the beach and swimming my fun in those childhood days revolved mainly around playing out with the other kids in the village. Indoors my great pleasure was listening to the radio – or the wireless, as we called it. We had a big monster of a wooden radio set with a dry battery inside and an accumulator. The set bore the wartime Utility label. I occasionally had to take the accumulator down into the village to have it charged. I did not know exactly what that meant but everyone knew that you had to get your accumulator charged. These days you sometimes see these old wireless sets on television programmes like *Bargain Hunt* or *The Antiques Roadshow*. I wonder what became of our old set.

I loved the wireless. I really thought it was fantastic. We used to listen as a family; my favourite shows included the comedy programme, *ITMA* (It's That Man Again) starring Tommy Handley, Jack Train, Dorothy Summers and Molly Weir with their own special characters like Colonel Chinstrap and Mrs Mopp each of them had their regular spot in the show each week and their own special catchphrases: 'Can I do you now Sir?' or 'I don't mind if I do!'

I also enjoyed the weekly visit to *Much Binding In The Marsh* which was a comedy half-hour starring Richard Murdoch, Kenneth Horne and Sam Costa in a show set on an RAF station. Then there was Much Binding's army equivalent *Stand Easy* starring 'Cheerful' Charlie Chester and a navy equivalent starring Eric Barker.

Another great favourite of mine was a programme called *Happydrome* starring Harry Korris. The show was famous for his song *Ramsbottom and Enoch and me!* I loved my comedy even then. I also used to love the variety programmes, including Sunday evening's *Variety Bandbox* a weekly variety show; there was plenty of comedy on offer on that. The line up of artistes who appeared on the show reads like a 'Who's Who' of the radio stars of those days. It regularly featured comedians like Ted Ray, Derek Roy, Frankie Howerd, Tony Hancock, Max Wall, Suzette Tarri, Al Read and Arthur English as well as popular singers like Petula Clarke, Dorothy Squires, David Hughes, Issy Bonn and Anne Shelton. The show even had a big band spot every week which featured bands and orchestras led by Ted Heath, Harry Roy, Geraldo, Ambrose, Joe Loss and Edmundo Ros.

One of the most popular shows on the wireless was the cowboy variety show presented by Big Bill Campbell and his Rocky Mountain Rhythm, featuring 'The Sweet Voice of the West' Peggy Bailey who later became Big Bill Campbell's wife. This must have been my first introduction to country music.

But of all the programmes on the BBC at the time the one which was absolutely unmissable for a lad of eleven or twelve was the nightly fifteen minute episode of the radio thriller *Dick Barton Special Agent* which was on at a quarter to seven each evening on the light programme. The series ran from 1946 to 1951 and when they took Dick, Jock and Snowy's adventures off the air and replaced the programme with *The Archers* I cried. I literally cried! All I had was an occasional Paul Temple adventure on the wireless but it was not as thrilling as my daily ration of Dick, Jock and Snowy!

As far as reading was concerned I had no interest in comics. There were plenty about like *The Beano*, *The Dandy* and *Comic Cuts*. There was also *Film Fun* and *Radio Fun* but I didn't care for any of these although I did give *The Eagle* a try for a little while when it first came out in 1950 with Dan Dare *Pilot of the Future* on the front cover and his arch-enemy The Mekon!

My reading matter was on a much higher level than Desperate Dan, Lord Snooty or Keyhole Kate. I was an avid reader of all four of the serialised story papers (they weren't comics!): *The Rover*, *The Wizard*, *The Adventure* and *The Hotspur*. Every week I would spend some of my paper delivery money on these four boys' magazines. I would read them from cover to cover, right through to the inevitable cliff-hanger ending of each story and I remember being thrilled by the exploits of the amazing *Wilson of the Wizard*, Alf Tupper – *The Tough of the Track*, and the brilliant football stars *Baldy Hogan* and *Limp Along Leslie*!

The war started when I was three years old and lasted until I was nine. I do remember bits about the war; I remember Mum having ration books and clothing and sweet coupons. I clearly recall the sound of the air raid siren and the 'all clear' and we had a Morrison air raid shelter in our kitchen which we all had to crawl into when the siren went. It was like a huge reinforced metal box with the sides missing. The top was our dining table. We felt safe in there waiting for the 'all clear'. Best of all, I remember the end of the war when we had a huge bonfire in the village on VE Day. But instead of Guy Fawkes on it we had an effigy of Hitler with his swastika armband. The baked potatoes cooked in the ashes were just brilliant.

School examinations were not called the eleven-plus then. It was called the scholarship and there were just two of us from our year who passed the scholarship to go up to Barry County Grammar School, Denise Bassett (the daughter of Rhoose School's Headmaster) and me! Though I loved my time at Rhoose School I certainly didn't enjoy my time at Barry Grammar School. For some reason I hated the classwork and was far more interested in sport. I played for the school first XI at cricket and I followed and supported the school rugby team, but as for the schoolwork, I preferred to forget it.

Several years after my time at that school a new school was built in another part of Barry to replace it. The old school grounds and buildings were sold to developers; my old cricket field and running track have now got a couple of hundred houses on them. In fact my niece Jacqueline lives opposite the old school and the main classroom block and Science Lab is now a Marston's pub-restaurant. I left school in 1952 with a couple of O-levels and a happy heart.

CHAPTER 2

First Visit to London

On leaving school I had made up my mind that I wanted to join the Royal Air Force. I did not know what I wanted to do in the RAF but I felt an affinity to it, probably through living just two miles from the largest RAF station in the UK, RAF St Athan. During the war RAF St Athan as the largest station was very high profile and attracted many distinguished visitors, including HM King George VI and Queen Elizabeth, Prince Bernhard of The Netherlands and France's General De Gaulle. As children we were permitted to go onto the camp at St Athan for just two purposes; they allowed us to go to the Astra Cinema on the camp and we were also allowed to go into a large drill shed which had been converted into a roller skating rink. That was much better than skating on the road in Aberthaw. I suppose things like this and the visiting dignitaries gave the Air Force a certain attraction but I do not know if that is the reason I wanted to join. I suppose I just fancied it, so I sent away my application to join the RAF as an apprentice.

Whilst I was waiting for the application to go through I got myself a temporary job at a local electrical and music retailer in Barry; helping their engineer to install TV sets. We would visit customers all over the area and put up 'H' and 'X' aerials on their houses and then tune in their TV sets to the local Wenvoe television mast which was located just outside Cardiff. Of course this was for the elite few who could afford a television in 1952. We did this work throughout the week from Monday to Friday, but we didn't install TV's on a Saturday for some reason so on that day I was required to help in the shop.

They put me in the records and sheet music department which was just perfect for me. It enabled me to keep right up to date with what was going on across the music scene and in the new charts. I remember well the record charts, which had started at the end of 1952. The very first chart was topped by Al Martino singing *Here in my Heart*. Prior to this the charts were always calculated not on record sales but on sales of sheet music. This had been an unsatisfactory system and the record charts which replaced it led to a massive increase of interest in records and sales of 45's.

Before I could be accepted for the RAF apprenticeship it was necessary for me to undergo various aptitude tests and medical examinations; I was to travel for these tests to RAF Halton near Wendover in Buckinghamshire. I had been sent a railway warrant to get me to Halton where the tests were spread over a couple of days with two overnight stays. When all the tests were over in order to get back home to South Wales I needed to take a train from Wendover to London and change trains to get another train to Cardiff, then from there one down the vale to Aberthaw.

I had never been to London before; I decided that I would break my journey there because I was very keen to see London and particularly the London Palladium. As a child Mum and Dad occasionally took me to the New Theatre in Cardiff to see variety shows as they were great theatre fans; to go to the theatre was a great thrill. The internationally famous London Palladium was legendary even then, some years before TV's *Sunday Night at the London Palladium* hosted by Tommy Trinder, and later Bruce Forsyth. The thought that I had the chance to actually see the fantastic London Palladium was too good to miss.

I got to the Palladium about lunchtime and although it was good to see the famous theatre I was a bit disappointed at first: Argyle Street where the theatre is located turned out to be just a very ordinary unimpressive side street. Not at all how I had imagined it. However when I got a look inside the theatre was everything I had imagined it to be. Even when empty it seemed to have an aura; an atmosphere which was practically tangible. But what did make me sit up and take notice was that there was an afternoon matinee performance advertised for that very day, and top of the bill was one of my favourite singers: Tennessee Ernie Ford. Wow! Tennessee Ernie.

The theatre had seats available in the stalls (very expensive), in the Dress Circle (very expensive), in the Upper Circle (still expensive) and right at the top – above the Upper Circle – the Balcony, otherwise known as 'the gods'. I could afford the three shillings (15p in today's money) to get a seat up there for the afternoon matinee performance.

What a great thrill to be actually sitting in one of the 2,200 seats inside this amazing theatre, to see Tennessee Ernie Ford –*Shotgun Boogie* and all that. It was a full variety show with the great Tennessee Ernie closing the show. After the overture by the pit orchestra the first act on stage was a black tap-dancing duo called The Clark Brothers who were brilliant. Then it was time for comedy and who should come on stage but a comedy duo at an early stage in their career – Morecambe and Wise - you may have heard of them! It was a fantastic show right through and it was a terrific experience for the princely sum of three shillings.

Tennessee Ernie was quite memorable and seemed larger than life, singing his great hits *Smokey Mountain Boogie*, *Sixteen Tons*, *Mule Train* and of course *Shotgun Boogie*. He did not have his biggest hit in the UK until three years later in March 1955 when *Give Me Your Word* shot up to number one in the charts and remained there for seven weeks.

Since then the Palladium has always remained my favourite theatre. Jean and I have been there to see many shows over the years including *Chitty Chitty Bang Bang* with Michael Ball, the incredible *Scrooge – the Musical* starring Tommy Steele, and other great musicals like *Sister Act* with Sheila Hancock, *Oliver* and *Joseph and his Amazing Technicolor Dreamcoat*.

Thrilled by the chance to see Tennessee Ernie I was still excited all the way back home on the train to South Wales; I couldn't wait to tell my folks that I had seen a show at the famous London Palladium.

My first visit to London had been a highly memorable one.

CHAPTER 3

RAF Aircraft Apprentice

On 29th April 1953 at the age of seventeen I became a member of Her Majesty's Royal Air Force as an aircraft apprentice training to be a ground radar fitter to service and repair radar installations on airfields – as opposed to an air radar fitter who would service the parts of the radar equipment located on board the aircraft. The apprenticeship was a three year course at RAF Locking just outside Weston-super-Mare in Somerset. I was in the 74th entry of aircraft apprentices, RAF Locking. I was advised it was going to be like being back in school; most of the course was classroom work with workshops containing radar equipment for us to familiarise ourselves with the actual gear we would be working on. With occasional field trips to airfields during term time. There would also be work in the gymnasium and on the parade ground among other things.

For the first five weeks of the course we did not see anything to do with radar, or any text books or even any classrooms. These things were not even mentioned. On the first day after we checked into our billets we were all issued with our uniforms and kit. On the second day we were all scalped with a service haircut and for the rest of the five weeks we did drill. Our education started by getting to know every square inch of the parade ground as we learned what square-bashing was. We were confined to camp for that first five weeks without any off camp passes, even at weekends.

Our first respite came when we had a five day mid term leave which coincided with the Queen's Coronation. I took the train home to Aberthaw to spend the break with my family and on Coronation Day June 2nd I went to visit a pal of mine in the village who was a bit of an electronics wizard and had a huge shed in his garden full of technical gear. We settled down and watched the Coronation together on a little four-inch screen on one of these bits of equipment in my pal's shed!

It was soon back to camp to start the course proper and though there was still a bit of square-bashing to do the course itself was enjoyable. In fact practically the whole time I spent at Locking was most enjoyable; the course was a challenge but I loved it.

I played football for the station team in the local North Somerset League, and cricket for the station first XI. There was no local league but we played invitation matches against other RAF stations, colleges and universities. We enjoyed one memorable day at the county ground in Taunton, home of Somerset County Cricket Club, when we were matched against Somerset 2nd XI. A bit of a mismatch because we got hammered, but a wonderful experience to play on such a superb ground. Whenever I see Somerset at home on TV playing at Taunton – whoever I am with I say, 'I've played there!' We had a similar great day when we played against Bristol University on their lovely ground, which is also occasionally used by Somerset County Cricket Club.

I was keen on all sports, including cycling and I joined the RAF Locking Cycling Club. I took part in many of the twenty-five mile cycle races which the club held on courses in the hills around Banwell and the Cheddar Gorge. But the cycling I enjoyed most was during our extended summer leave from our course when together with one of my RAF apprentice pals, Jim Cornwell, we would go youth hostelling for a couple of weeks.

I particularly enjoyed the trip one summer when we started at my home in Aberthaw and cycled through the Vale of Glamorgan, along the South Wales coast to the Gower Peninsular, stopping at a hostel at the end of the peninsular at Port Eynon where we spent a couple of nights. From Port Eynon we continued down the coast to stay a night near Tenby before cycling on to the city of St Davids where we spent another couple of nights and taking the opportunity to visit the stunning cathedral. After that we headed back inland. We took three or four days to get back to base via the Brecon Beacons and down through the valleys back to Aberthaw. After spending so much time in uniform and studying every day this was a complete change from our daily routine and a memorable holiday for two lads who were still teenagers!

I lost track with Jim after we left Locking. We had both moved around a lot at home and abroad on different postings in the service and we lost touch with each other. Then surprisingly in the mid nineties I received a phone call from him. I couldn't believe it was him at first because the person I was talking to sounded as though he came from Sydney or Melbourne. When I knew him Jim came from Hampshire, and he sounded like he came from Hampshire! It turned out that he had emigrated to Australia, bought some land out in the bush, built himself a farmhouse with his own hands and settled there with his wife and family. He had come back to England to finalise the estate of his father who had just died. He had tracked me down and said he was only a hundred miles away and he was coming to visit me.

What a reunion! Neither of us had a clue as to what life had brought the other; after going out for a meal we returned home and sat up nearly all night reminiscing. He was flying home to Australia the next day but what an unforgettable reunion it was. I spent the next few days telling Jean about all our adventures when we were together in the RAF apprentices at Locking - and there were many of those! It had been a wonderful surprise.

Locking camp is only about four miles from the old fashioned seaside resort of Weston-super-Mare. For the first year of our time at Locking we were only allowed off camp at weekends. Monday to Thursday we had to remain on camp. After a year this rule was relaxed, allowing us off camp every evening and all day on Saturdays and Sundays – but only in uniform. Only in our final year were we allowed to wear civilian clothes when we were off duty.

I have always loved the seaside, and I loved Weston with its long promenade, the Grand Pier and the Winter Gardens where we used to go dancing and talent spotting. They used to have a ten or twelve piece orchestra playing for dancing in the Winter Gardens every Wednesday and Saturday. Proper ballroom dancing too! There was an outdoor and an indoor swimming pool on the front; it was just a great place to spend some time. We were worked pretty hard on the course at Locking and it was good to have somewhere like Weston where we could relax on our time off.

When I had been at Locking about a year the station band were looking for new members. I thought this might be for me so I joined. The band was in two parts – a trumpet band and a pipe band with a joint rhythm section of snare drums, tenor drums, bass drum and cymbals. As I could not play any of these things they started me off on cymbals, probably where I could do the least damage. I set myself the task of learning the bagpipes and I spent about three months wrestling with this alien instrument before I got the hang of it in the end. So much so that when the RAF Locking apprentices station band was selected to appear at the Royal Tournament at Earl's Court, London I was among the musicians marching up and down playing *Scotland the Brave* etc. Quite a thrill.

Every year at Locking the three entries which had completed a full year of the course were rewarded with the rare treat of two weeks summer camp at Saunton Sands, near Braunton in North Devon. We were accommodated in two-man bivouacs on the beach and it was a great break from the classroom, with a mobile cookhouse which ensured we didn't starve.

There was much excitement at Locking one time while I was there; it was announced that we were going to have a visit to the station by the Queen's sister, Princess Margaret. For about three or four weeks before the visit the old service instruction came into force – 'If it moves, move it. If it doesn't move, paint it!' You would not believe how much white paint was used in the weeks before the royal visit. And green paint as well because if anyone painting the kerbstones splashed white paint on to the grass they would have to cover it up with green paint. Unbelievable but true, because for a royal visit the grass had to be green, not splashed with white paint!

We were all in our 'best blue' on the day of the visit and in formation on the parade ground, to be inspected by Princess Margaret (which meant she just walked past us) along with the camp's top brass – Station Commander etc. As a result of the visit my only lasting memory of this short brush with royalty is just how small Princess Margaret was. A very attractive but very tiny lady.

For me personally a great advantage of being stationed at Locking was the fact that Weston-super-Mare was one of the ports of call for the Campbell's Steamers (later known as the White Funnel Fleet). This excellent fleet of paddle-steamers ran regular services across the Bristol Channel between Ilfracombe in North Devon and Weston-super-Mare on the English side and Cardiff, Penarth and Barry, just five miles from my home in Aberthaw, on the Welsh side, so they were very convenient for me on weekends off.

From April to October each year there was a daily ferry service, so anytime I had a weekend pass I took advantage of the fact that it was much easier for me to get the ferry instead of the train. The journey on the train would have meant going via Bristol Temple Meads, the Severn Tunnel and changing again at Cardiff. So I became a regular on these cross channel ferries, *The Cardiff Queen*, *The Bristol Queen* and *The Ravenswood*. On a Friday evening I would get off the ferry at Cardiff, Penarth or Barry then hitch-hike the ten or twelve miles home to Aberthaw, returning on the Sunday evening.

The only downside of my time at Locking was that I entered in the 74th entry, but spent so much time in hospital in my final year with a chronic throat problem that I practically lived in Wroughton RAF Hospital near Swindon. I was scheduled to have my tonsils removed, but they were not able to operate because of a heavy infection which just went on and on. I missed so much of the course that I was moved down two entries and passed out at the end of 1956 with the 76th entry, a qualified ground radar fitter with the rank of Junior Technician.

I eventually had my tonsils removed in 1962 when I was twenty six at the RAF Hospital, Ely in Cambridgeshire. It is a simple operation for a child but when you are an adult it blinking well hurts! After the operation I found myself struggling to eat jelly and other easily swallowed stuff while kids in the same ward were tucking in to toast and crisps. I felt like a right wimp.

CHAPTER 4

Somerset to Shropshire

After passing out at the end of my apprenticeship I had a fortnight's leave before taking up my first posting which was to a station just twenty-five miles away from Locking: RAF Weston Zoyland near Bridgwater, Somerset. Posted there with me was a pal from the 76th entry at Locking, Eric Ellis. It was a bit disappointing not to be seeing another part of the country. I had been over three and a half years in Somerset and nice as it was I was ready for a change of scenery – not a posting twenty-five miles away! Still as things turned out, it wasn't going to be for long.

Eric and I arrived at Weston Zoyland in January 1957; it was a strange posting for us. Yes, there was radar equipment on the airfield for us to service but aircraft movements were very few and far between, and there was little work for us to do. Weston Zoyland had been used primarily as a transport airfield in the war by both the RAF and the United States Army Air Forces. After the war it was used as a reserve RAF Fighter Command airfield until the station eventually closed in 1958.

Whilst we were there the station was essentially in the process of closing down; our stay only lasted for a few months before Eric and I were both promoted to Corporal and posted together to RAF Ternhill near Market Drayton in Shropshire in the May of 1957. A posting which changed my life forever in two ways. Firstly and most importantly I met and married the person I was going to spend the rest of my life with. Secondly, it is true that I was only at RAF Ternhill for barely twelve months but it was during this time that I got my very first experience of singing to an audience for money! I know it was only in a little skiffle group in a small pub but it was the beginning of something that eventually took over my life completely, becoming a career and opening the doors to many friendships and good things throughout my life.

RAF Ternhill was just a dormitory station for us. We were only based there for our accommodation; our actual working days were spent about eighteen miles away at an isolated radar station in the hills of Staffordshire near Newcastle-under-Lyme. Our work station was called RAF Camp Hill North.

We were only a small team at Camp Hill North. We were involved in surveillance work and there were about forty people working on the site. We were stationed there for nearly a year. Each day a Land Rover would pick us up from our billets at Ternhill and take us to work and to deliver us back at the end of the day. With so few of us in our unit we all got to know each other very well and it was a terrific atmosphere in which to work.

While I was at Ternhill a couple of my work colleagues were keen tennis players. I had played a little in the past but because of their keenness I really got into it and played a lot with them, and found it very enjoyable. One of them, John, was married with four sons and his wife was expecting again, obviously hoping for a daughter. We were actually playing tennis when the news came through that his wife had given birth to triplets – three boys! Imagine that! He was immediately given compassionate leave and by the time he returned to camp a couple of weeks later he had just about come to terms with it.

Another thing I did when I was posted to Ternhill was to treat myself to a new piano accordion so that I could keep my hand in. I hadn't played at all in my time at Locking and Weston Zoyland so I was very rusty. I could not practice in the barrack room so I used to go to one of the drying rooms in our accommodation block where we did our laundry and I would practice there out of earshot of any non-music lovers! (or probably it should be any music lovers!) I would spend at least a couple of hours at a time in there honing my skills!

It was during one of these practice sessions a chap walked in and told me he played guitar. He said his name was Jimmy Dunlop and would I mind if he joined me? We chatted and he asked me if I sang. I said, 'Yes I do.' A week or two later he called in again and made a proposition to me. He said he had a mate, Tex, who was an RAF policeman. Tex played guitar and sang and the two of them had been to The Star, a pub in Market Drayton and been offered a job singing there if they could put a skiffle group together. Evidently there were three other pubs in the town with skiffle groups; they were all doing great business and The Star wanted to do the same. I told him I was up for it and he said he knew a couple of local lads who would join us – one on a snare drum and the other one on a tea-chest bass.

We had a couple of quick rehearsals in my drying room and once we thought we could do it we all went and saw the landlord Mr Tom Gregory, who offered us the job. Mr Gregory offered us five evenings a week – Tuesday through to Saturday. He had found out that the going rate for a skiffle group was £2-10 shillings a night which was ten bob a night each (50p in today's money.) In addition to that they would take the tin round every night and we would share the proceeds at the end of the week. It turned out that this usually amounted to another ten bob each, so personally, I was picking up £3 for the five evenings and our beer was free!

This may not sound a lot but this was 1957; my service pay as a Corporal in the RAF was four guineas a week – or £4.20. So by playing in the skiffle group this almost doubled my week's wages – it was great fun too! And this was an important milestone – my first ever professional engagement. I could not believe it – I was playing music for money!

Skiffle was a great craze at the time and it was spin-off from the popularity of traditional jazz, where Lonnie (Tony) Donegan played guitar and banjo in a top traditional jazz band with Chris Barber on trombone and the bandleader Ken Colyer on trumpet. In all of the band's live bookings they always included what they called a skiffle segment, with Lonnie singing, accompanied by his own guitar, a washboard and tea-chest bass. From this came his recording of *Rock Island Line* which started the whole skiffle craze. In no time there were thousands of skiffle groups all over the country – including ours in The Star at Market Drayton. We sang all the skiffle hits by Donegan (*Rock Island Line, Lost John, Gambling Man* and *Puttin' on the Style* etc.), the Vipers, Chas McDevitt and Nancy Whiskey (*Freight Train* and *Green Back Dollar* etc.) and many more. We also included American folk songs like *Frankie and Johnnie* and *Wabash Cannonball* as well as a few novelty numbers like the Shel Silverstein number

I'm Satisfied with my Girl and *T'aint no sin to take off your skin and dance around in your bones!*, later covered by Tom Waits. We had fun!

I am pleased to say - there turned out to be other benefits as well. A couple of girls called in the pub one Saturday night in September when we were playing. They were on their way to a dance in Market Drayton Town Hall. They stayed a little while and during our break we got chatting to them – in fact I made a date with one of them to meet her the following night, on the Sunday. I must have been pretty irresistible, being a fit eleven stone with a stunning crew cut! The girl's name was Jean and she lived ten miles away in Whitchurch. The following evening I got on my trusty bike and cycled there to meet her; we spent the evening together having a drink and chatting and enjoying each other's company. I could not wait to see her again. We must have got on really well because we arranged to meet again a few days later and it might sound impulsive but I actually proposed to her on that first date. I remember her reply. It was, 'Don't be so daft!' But I persevered and eventually she said, 'Yes.' It must have taken me all of a fortnight to persuade her. It sounds unbelievable but it is true. Over the next few months that trusty Raleigh Lenton bicycle of mine did a lot of mileage back and forth between Ternhill and Whitchurch!

Jean and I were married just six months after our first date, on the 22nd of March 1958 at St Alkmund's Church, Whitchurch, with Eric Ellis as my best man. The wedding was at eleven O'clock in the morning and at four in the afternoon we were on the train to Brighton for a week's honeymoon. We stayed for the week at a huge hotel, which was well known as a honeymoon hotel, the Ocean Hotel, Saltdean, near Brighton, where we were astonished to find ourselves in the company of over a hundred other couples from around the country who had got married on the same day!

At the time when Jean and I got married I was already on what were known as PWR's – A pre-warning roster of an imminent posting abroad. This meant that I could expect to have an overseas posting within the following twelve months. When we were first married we lived for a short while with Jean's sister Eileen and her family in Market Drayton. It was only one month into our marriage when notice of my posting came through. It was going to be an accompanied posting to an RAF station in Germany. An accompanied posting means the serviceman's family can join him for the duration of the posting. I left on my own at the end of April for Germany; Jean was to follow later after our accommodation in married quarters had been arranged.

My twelve months at RAF Ternhill had certainly been an eventful and possibly the most important year of my life.

CHAPTER 5

Germany

My posting abroad took me to RAF Goch in Germany, just on the border with The Netherlands near Nijmegen. On arrival I immediately applied for married quarters. There were none available for about three months but a friend of mine at work, Doug Marchant, and his wife were already in married quarters in the town of Goch. They very kindly offered to put Jean and me up for a short while until we got a home of our own. So Jean was able to follow me to Germany after a couple of months and we spent a very happy two and a half years there. After staying with Doug and Lil for a month we were allocated our own house where we lived for the rest of our time in Germany. The married quarters at Goch were two and three bedroom houses in three adjacent streets in the middle of town: Nierstrasse, Feldstrasse and Wiesenstrasse. We were given No. 70 Feldstrasse and suddenly we found ourselves as a normal married couple with our own front door. We settled in really well and loved being in the local environment. Sometimes you find that married quarters are a bit too close to work, occupied by all service families and you are all in a little service world of your own. It was different here. We just felt that we were a part of the little town itself. We were welcomed by the locals and we had our own milkman and a local pub. We really felt a part of the community.

Shortly after Jean joined me in Goch we decided that we would need a car to get about. Our nearest big city was Dusseldorf about fifty miles away and we went to a dealership there which had been recommended to us. We bought our very first car – a second hand 1958 white Ford Prefect which was just six months old and was our pride and joy. We paid £320 for it on the never-never. It was about a tenner a month! I quickly had to learn to drive and after about a month I passed my test and obtained an International Driving Licence. So we were now raring to go and to discover Germany and The Netherlands. There were plenty of places we wanted to visit; we were determined to make the most of our time living in Germany. Before Jean joined me I had been on a trip to the extraordinary city of Amsterdam and the Amstel Brewery; I had already earmarked this as a city I would love to take Jean to see. It really is a beautiful place. We have been there many times since, and never tire of it. We did our day to day shopping locally but things like groceries, fresh meat and vegetables were cheaper in The Netherlands so once every two or three weeks we would get in the car and have an afternoon in Nijmegen, which was about twenty-five miles away, to do a big shopping session. One thing we did find strange was asking for a kilo of eggs instead of a dozen or half a dozen. A kilo is usually about sixteen or seventeen eggs depending on the size of them. If you really think about it, it makes sense! We found Nijmegen to be a lovely city to visit and we enjoyed spending some time there. It is packed with beautiful historic buildings and has two or three lovely parks.

Having the car gave us a great chance to visit many tourist places in this lovely part of Germany with its proximity to the River Rhine. The two lovely cities of Dusseldorf and Cologne were well within reach but just to drive around the countryside was a delight. We visited many places in neighbouring Netherlands such as the famous Keukenhof bulb fields near Amsterdam, The Hague, Arnhem, The Zuyder Zee and of course Amsterdam itself.

The kind of music that was prevalent at the time in Germany was Dixieland and traditional jazz. There were loads of traditional jazz bands about and skiffle was also very popular. As far as my music was concerned our area was overloaded with skiffle groups so that was out. However Doug Marchant, who we lived with at first, was a musician himself and knew that I played and sang. I had a chance meeting with a friend of his from work, Jock Forrest, who was a telephonist on camp and also played drums. Jock revealed he was looking to put a dance band together and said that Doug had told him about me. He asked if I would be interested. Evidently there was not a band around who could play for dances in officers' and sergeants' messes and for official functions. I told Jock I would certainly love to be involved. He also managed to recruit an excellent piano player, Gordon Rutter, plus Ken Leverett on trumpet and Doug Marchant on trombone. We had a few weeks of rehearsals in the evenings and then we felt we were ready to offer our services as a dance band, playing quicksteps, waltzes, foxtrots etc. and throwing in a bit of rock and roll and party dances. We called our band The Tramps not because of the way we looked but because of our signature tune, the Rodgers and Hart classic *The Lady is a Tramp.*

The Tramps played about one night a week. It was usually a Saturday or an occasional Friday; after taking a little while to become known and established we were installed as the official dance band for all the officers' and sergeants' messes in West Germany. We played at RAF stations like Goch, Laarbruch, Bruggen, Wildenrath and many others all over Germany, as well as for army units and for civic functions. We played for US Air Force units and on one occasion we even played for a ball at the American Embassy in The Hague.

By far the most important event during the time we were in Germany was the birth of our daughter, Lynne Denise, at the RAF Hospital Wegberg, near Munchen Gladbach on 15th April, 1959. Wegberg was the nearest service hospital to where we lived. It was about fifty miles away. The funny thing is that I remember my Dad's last words to us as we left to go to Germany, – 'Don't you go bringing any little "Jerries" back when you come home!' Sorry Dad!

Lynne spent the first fourteen months of her life with us at Goch until the end of my tour in 1960 and a posting back to the UK.

Our next door neighbours in Feldstrasse were a delightful couple from Fife in Scotland, a Sergeant and his wife Jock and Helen Wallace. They were quite a bit older than us and Helen simply doted on our new baby, Lynne; she was like a second Mum to Jean and such a great help with the baby. They were posted back to the UK when Lynne was about six months old and we lost touch, and sadly have never seen them since, but we certainly won't forget them. That's service life I suppose.

We really loved our time in Germany and had always longed to go back there to see it again so about eight years ago we went back to visit the place just for old time's sake. We took the car and drove across country to Harwich in Essex, from where we took a ferry to the Hook of Holland. We stayed a night in a hotel there before driving over to Goch, a distance of about a hundred miles. We booked in to a nice hotel in Goch for three or four days, using restaurants we used to know, and paying a visit to our old house. We found that Goch was just identical to the way we remembered it; it hadn't changed at all. It seemed as though just a few days had gone by instead of the fifty years that it actually was.

The three streets in which the married quarters were situated were of course still there but the houses were all completely empty and by the looks of it they had been left unoccupied for a considerable time. The grass outside was chest high and there was no sign of life at all. The houses had all been the property of the British Ministry of Defence and when RAF Goch closed down a couple of years earlier all the occupants of the houses went back to the UK. Then the houses were all locked up until it could be decided what to do with them. A couple of months before our visit they were bought from the MOD by the local Goch Town Council to be let to local residents.

We walked though the long grass up to our old house and peered through the window. What astounded us was that inside the house all the carpets, light fittings and everything were still in place and on the outside of the houses there was no sign of any graffiti or vandalism. There were no squatters or anything like that. It was amazing, but it was great to see the respect which these properties had received since being vacated - and it was a real eye opener.

Whilst we were staying in Goch we paid a visit to one of our favourite places on the River Rhine, the little town of Rees. It is about fifteen miles from Goch and when we lived there we would often spend many a pleasant afternoon in Rees. It was right alongside the river and it even had a little sandy beach where we could sit on a sunny day with baby Lynne in her carrycot; we loved it. The Rhine was a very busy river and a main thoroughfare for huge barges carrying thousands of containers to the docks at Rotterdam. We could also sit and relax and watch the many pleasure cruisers on the river. It was a delight to go back there and to reminisce.

We also took time out to visit the Reichwald War Cemetery near Kleve, less than ten miles from Goch, which is looked after by the War Graves Commission. Though it is very sad to see the memorials to over seven thousand British and Commonwealth servicemen buried there the commission deserved high praise for the wonderful care and attention they give to this amazing site. The way it is lovingly looked after must be a great comfort to visiting relatives of these men who gave their lives in the service of the country; it is beautiful.

After our visit to Goch, we motored over to Nijmegen, the town where we used to do our shopping. We spent an afternoon there and over the next couple of days travelled in a leisurely way back to the Hook of Holland for the ferry then home. It was a fantastic nostalgic experience for both of us, harking back to our time there fifty years previously. It is something we would both love to do again.

As the time approached for my tour of duty in Germany to come to an end we speculated on where we might be posted on return to the UK. The details finally came through: I was to be posted to RAF Marham near Kings Lynn in Norfolk. I had never been to this part of England before so it was going to be a totally new experience. It was August 1960 when we left Germany. We loaded up the car for the drive back to the UK; I had a fortnight's repatriation leave before I had to report to RAF Marham and we stayed with Mum and Dad in South Wales for this short break.

CHAPTER 6

East Anglia

I had been driving in Germany and The Netherlands on my International Driving Licence for about two years but this licence was not valid in the UK. I was only permitted to drive legally from Germany through The Netherlands and Belgium to the ferry in France. Upon arrival I was permitted to drive across England to South Wales until I reached the address I was to be staying at. As soon as I arrived at the address that was my first destination in the UK my International Driving Licence was no longer valid. I would have to put 'L' plates on the car and not drive without a qualified driver accompanying me until I passed my UK driving test! It sounds crazy but evidently that was the law. Luckily I had known about this situation long before I left Germany so I had made prior arrangements to have my test a week after arriving in Aberthaw. My driving test was in Bridgend, about fourteen miles away. My brother accompanied me to the testing station. Fortunately I had no problem with the test and I duly received my pink slip, threw away my 'L' plates I had been displaying for six days and suddenly I was legal again. They call it bureaucracy and it is something we just have to put up with.

Our journey home from Germany to South Wales was a particularly uncomfortable one for Jean. She was seven months pregnant, and was suffering very badly from morning sickness. The sickness had started very early in the pregnancy and it persisted almost to the end. The road journey of over four hundred miles, plus the ferry journey across the English Channel meant that we were in transit for well over twelve hours. This made it very difficult for her, especially with the sixteen month old Lynne to look after as well. Still, we made it, and it was nice to get back to the family, to be able to spend a couple of weeks with them.

When my leave was up I drove across to Norfolk; Jean and Lynne stayed with my Mum in South Wales until I was able to arrange some accommodation for us at my new station. I checked into my new place of work, RAF Marham, to find that my job was going to be servicing the radar landing system on a very busy airfield. Marham was the home of a large number of Valiants, part of the RAF's V-Bomber fleet. After a couple of false alarms our son Kenneth Mark was born on 19th October 1960, at RAF Hospital St. Athan about two miles from my old home in Aberthaw. I had only been at RAF Marham a short while before I took a week's leave to come back to South Wales to see my new son.

At Marham they had an airfield radar system which was unfamiliar to me so after a month or so I was enrolled on a four week course back to RAF Locking in Somerset for a specialist training period on this particular radar installation. After the course the powers that be decided that now I was fully trained as an expert on this system I would be screened at Marham. Screening meant that I could not be posted from there for at least the next five years. I did not really mind this; it meant that as a family we could settle in the area and put down some roots for a while.

When I arrived at Marham I had immediately applied for married quarters. Unfortunately there were none available for us straight away. When this happens the service has a policy of renting 'hirings', private houses near the camp in which they accommodate servicemen and their families until married quarters become available. We spent just over a year waiting and for that time we were allocated a hiring in the middle of Kings Lynn, twelve miles away. For the rest of our time at Marham we were allocated a married quarter which was a three bedroom house adjacent to the camp. King's Lynn is a very nice little market town with an excellent street market every Tuesday and Saturday. It was a nice place to live. I used to support the local football team, The Linnets and I used to entertain in the pub at the end of our street, The Bowling Green. When I went back to do a booking in King's Lynn about fifteen years ago I looked for the pub and could not find it; I was told it had been demolished to make way for more houses.

During my time there I found plenty of chances to continue with my music. I played at several pubs and clubs in the area, including a regular midweek booking in one of the three pubs in Marham

Village - The Coach and Horses. I also played at various venues in Kings Lynn, Swaffham, Castleacre, Hunstanton and I was a regular entertainer on Saturday evenings at The Greyhound in Sutton Bridge near Spalding.

I did three summer seasons in the lovely resort of Hunstanton. This was in a social club on a caravan park on the beach road. It was called Searle's Caravan Park and it was quite small at the time. It has now grown into a massive five star holiday complex, now known as Searle's Leisure Resort, and it was recently named as one of the five best holiday parks in England in the Visit England Awards for Excellence. These days they have many star names providing their guests with entertainment. In the mid 1960s they had me!

All my gigs were solo bookings but on occasions a couple of lads who worked with me and who played guitars would come along and sit in. We had good times. One of the lads who used to join me when I was playing at the local pubs was a workmate, Derek 'Ginge' Head, who was also an ex-apprentice at Locking. Ginge played guitar and loved to come along and have a session. For the local gigs he often provided the transport by taking us in his Heinkel bubble car! To get into it we had to pull open the front of the car and clamber in. It was just big enough to take the two of us plus my accordion and his guitar. We would roll up at the local garage, ask the petrol pump attendant (yes, they had them then!) for, 'half a gallon of the worst!' and off we would go for the evening. It was fun; I wish there were photos of us in the loaded bubble car.

I had to leave Marham for a few months in 1964 when the whole airfield was closed for major runway repairs. For the first four weeks I was loaned out to RAF Honington near Bury St Edmunds in Suffolk. After this I was seconded out to RAF Holbeach, a bombing range on the Wash in Lincolnshire about thirty miles from Marham. This was a very small unit where I stayed on site during the week and went home to the family at Marham on weekends.

It was while I was at Holbeach I had one of my proudest moments ever. I was always a keen snooker player and while I was at Holbeach I used to play in the Long Sutton and District Snooker League. The league had an exhibition visit by top snooker professional and former world champion Fred Davis, brother of the legendary Joe

Davis. Three players from our league were selected to play a frame against the great man during this exhibition; I was honoured to be one of those three players and although I got slaughtered I can still brag and say, 'I actually played a frame of snooker against eight-times world champion, the great Fred Davis!'

I have always played sport and table tennis was a favourite of mine. I played regularly at the time and I was part of the station team. We had a decent team and we were playing in two leagues which covered the whole of Norfolk and a big part of Cambridgeshire, so we got to travel quite a lot around the area. I was selected to play for the county of Norfolk and also to represent RAF Bomber Command in their table tennis team.

One other sport which RAF Marham introduced me to was tenpin bowling. The station had a four lane tenpin bowling alley installed in the NAAFI complex of the camp. Whenever we had a bit of spare time it was very handy to be able to spend an hour there and to enjoy this sport that was new to me. Some of the lads took it very seriously and joined league teams but I just enjoyed it for fun.

Jean enjoyed it too, and if we were going anywhere on a shopping expedition we usually chose Peterborough because there was a twenty-four lane tenpin bowling centre there. Some years later when we lived in North Wales we would occasionally drive a couple of friends over one hundred miles to Wolverhampton to have a game. That was the nearest bowling centre to where we lived. We still play a game or two in our local tenpin centre in Shrewsbury. We were never going to be any good at it; we just enjoyed the atmosphere and the fun.

Jean and the family really enjoyed the time we spent in Norfolk. There are some very nice beaches on the North Norfolk coast and some lovely old fashioned resorts. We would visit Sheringham, Cromer, Wells-next-the-Sea, Holkham, and Hunstanton which the children loved. I suppose Hunstanton was our real favourite and our family visits there were all brought back to me many years later when I was on the road full time as an entertainer in the 1990s. I was booked several times to do shows at the town's beautiful Princess Theatre. Going to Hunstanton for those shows brought back many happy memories of when we were there in the 1960s. After living in Norfolk for over five years we were beginning to feel like locals.

We had certainly settled into a routine; we knew the area very well.

When you have been screened at an RAF station for five years you can be almost certain that your next posting will be overseas. This turned out to be the case with me; at the end of almost six years at Marham my next posting came through and it was to send me to Aden, in the Middle East.

CHAPTER 7

Up the Gulf

It was August 1966 when I boarded a VC10 aircraft at Heathrow Airport for the six hour flight to Aden. I knew I was only going to be there for a year so I looked upon it as a bit of an adventure. What was called The Aden Emergency had been going on since 1963 and I knew that it was not RAF policy to send families into war zones. So I thought, 'well it can't be that bad otherwise they wouldn't have made it an accompanied twelve month tour.' If it had been considered that there was too much of a danger the tour would have undoubtedly been an unaccompanied one. Two months later Jean, Lynne and Mark boarded a Britannia aircraft for the thirteen hour flight to Aden. (The Britannia is much, much slower than the VC10.) The family arrived in Aden on the afternoon of 19th October which was Mark's sixth birthday.

Aden was a port on the southern edge of the Arabian Peninsular, with fierce summers and winters which were almost as hot. I was stationed at No.131 MU (Maintenance Unit) at RAF Khormaksar and that was my base camp. The first thing that happened when we arrived in Aden was a massive and urgent security briefing. We were put in no doubt that all British personnel were in danger of terrorist attacks and that there were unsafe zones which were no-go areas. There were so-called safe zones but even in those we were instructed never to go alone but in twos and threes for the sake of our own safety. It was quite a scary briefing but they made it plain it was essential and advised those of us who were being joined by our families to put them in the picture as how to take special care in the prevailing situation. The most crucial piece of advice was that you should never go anywhere alone. These warnings were given with such force that we were in no doubt that they were serious, not just something that they dreamed up.

My actual work was going to be repairing and servicing radar units at British RAF airfields in the Persian Gulf at places like Muharraq, Sharjah, Dubai and Bahrain. On a regular basis they would fly me up the gulf to these units where I would stay two or three days before coming back to base. Where I would keep myself busy in a workshop at RAF Khormaksar until the next trip up the gulf. It turned out to be very varied and enjoyable work.

I was allocated a flat for myself and my family in the middle of the town of Maala which was a couple of miles from Khormaksar camp. The flat was in the middle of the Maala Strait, a busy shopping area, and it was a first floor flat above a number of shops. We were above a general store called The China Store. Lynne and Mark went to school a few miles away in Steamer Point. The school bus collected them and returned them each day. School times were eight in the morning only until lunchtime. The temperature in the afternoons was simply too hot for any sort of work, including schoolwork. My own working times were also eight in the morning until 1.00 pm, so all of our afternoons were free and nearly all of them were spent at the Steamer Point Lido, a swimming paradise where both Lynne and Mark learned to swim. It was a private sandy beach with a huge swimming area surrounded by the necessary shark net. It was a complete delight.

We used to keep in touch with the family at home in South Wales by means of reel to reel tape recorder messages. I had a Grundig TK5 reel to reel recorder which I had left at home so that Mum and Peg could use it. When I got to Aden I bought a little second hand recorder and a few three inch reels of recording tape – which recorded about half an hour on each side. Each month the four of us would record a message to send home. After some initial shyness Lynne and Mark would talk to their Nan and Auntie Peg and Jean and I would give them all our news. I would then post it off to the family. We did not get a recorded tape back. Mum did not fancy doing that, but she wrote us long letters instead.

Once again, during the Aden experience I continued my interest in my music. As I was only going to be there for a year I had decided to have a rest from entertaining. Whilst in Norfolk I had been singing three or four nights a week for the last four years so I thought I would have a rest, though I did take my accordion with me just to practise and keep my hand in. However circumstances conspired to change things. It was New Year's Eve 1966 and Jean and I managed to get a friend to look after Lynne and Mark while we went out for the evening to the Families Club at RAF Khormaksar. We were looking forward to enjoying a relaxing party evening in a social atmosphere with work colleagues and their wives, having a dance and seeing the New Year in before going back home to our flat in Maala. The curfew had been extended from midnight to 1am for that night.

By about 7pm there was absolutely no sign of a band turning up at the club and an announcement was made that a huge clanger had been dropped. Two members of the committee each thought the other had booked the band so in actual fact no band had been booked. They announced that they were going to try to find a disco at short notice.

A workmate of mine, Dusty Mullett and his wife were with us at the club. Dusty played guitar and he suggested that we might be able to do something. He rushed home for his guitar and to get my accordion. In the meantime I drove up to the local radio station AFBA – The Aden Forces Broadcasting Association, a place where I had done a bit of work previously. I asked them to let me go on air, which they did, and I invited any musicians to join us at the Families Club. A guitarist, bass player and a sax player turned up. What it all sounded like, heaven only knows, but we got through the night and everybody had a good time. We felt like the cavalry coming to the rescue.

A couple of days later at work Dusty said to me, 'If we could get a couple more musicians, we could put a little band together.' When we were at the Families Club I had been reminded of what I was missing so I jumped at the idea. That evening I went to AFBA Radio Station and they let me go on air once again. I asked on the radio if there were any musicians who fancied doing a few gigs. The next day I had a call from two Geordie lads, Jimmy Beryl and Mark Patterson, who were professional musicians with the Royal Northumberland Fusiliers Band, a regiment which was stationed in Aden. I invited them to come to our flat to have a talk about it.

They were very keen. These army lads were having a really hard time in Aden. They had so much in the way of guard duties and armed escorting duties to do. The fusiliers band was also involved with parades, civic functions and church parades etc. The RAF's daily routine was a walk in the park compared what these lads had to contend with. So they were looking for a bit of light relief. Jimmy played drums, and Mark, though he played several instruments, was great on the double bass. We got together for a couple of rehearsals in a local social club. The club was called The Hair of the Dog so we called our new band The Hairy Dogs!

We only did about one gig a week due to all our service commitments but we really enjoyed the gigs we did. Jimmy and Mark often brought along some of their mates from the fusiliers band who would sit in with us on a variety of instruments. Sometimes we were a seven or eight-piece band. This was fantastic fun. The gigs were always an early finish – no later than 11pm because of the curfew when no one was allowed on the streets or off camp between midnight and 6am. The lads had to be inside the wire by midnight and we also had to be indoors.

I did get an opportunity to have a short break from Aden at one time. I was selected for the Middle East Air Forces table tennis team to take part in a tour of Cyprus and Malta. Over the five days we were put up in RAF Akrotiri in Cyprus and RAF Luqa in Malta and we played teams from those stations and a few army bases. It was a most enjoyable tour and Jean never ceases to remind me how I deserted her in war-torn Aden to go and play ping-pong! I told her what a beautiful island Cyprus was – probably the only place I have ever been to where I could happily live, except of course the UK. I loved it and promised Jean and the family that I would take them there as soon as I could.

When I was working up the gulf Jean and the kids were still able to go to the lido as escorted buses went there regularly from Khormaksar and Maala. The escorts on the buses were army or Air Force personnel. This was necessary because although we were able to live a pretty normal life Aden was in the middle of troubled times. There had been a British presence in Aden since 1839 when a British territory was established there. The territory became a Crown Colony in 1931 and remained so happily for over thirty years until the rise of the National Liberation Front and by the mid sixties it was obvious that the British had to withdraw.

Aden became part of the People's Republic of South Yemen. Jean, Lynne and Mark left Aden to return to the UK in July 1967 and were given temporary accommodation in Wilmslow in Cheshire. I followed them home a month later, and was repatriated in the August. The last British troops left Aden in November 1967.

I know there were regular terrorist incidents, and all of us had to take our turns doing guard duties and security. Despite all of this we had a wonderful time, and our time in Aden was a very positive experience for me and my family, certainly a great learning experience for the children as well as for Jean and me. But it was good to be home in the UK again and to see a bit of greenery instead of all that sand. I will never forget my first sight of land in England from that aircraft coming home from Aden. It was just the green, everything looked green. We had not seen anything green for a year!

CHAPTER 8

Hello Civvy Street

On my return from Aden I was posted to RAF Valley near Holyhead on the beautiful Isle of Anglesey at the northwest tip of North Wales. We were allocated married quarters in the village of Caergeiliog about a mile from the camp. Lynne and Mark went to school at Caegeiliog Primary School. My work was to service and repair the radar equipment on the airfield and in the control tower, where I was based. I was conversant with the airfield equipment and with that in the control tower as it was the same installation as we had at Marham, so settling into the job was no problem.

I spent my final year in the Royal Air Force working on this equipment until my demob from the service in August 1968. I had enjoyed my life in the Air Force, but I was more than ready for a change, yet the prospect of civilian life was something I was quite nervous about. For fifteen years I had been cosseted in the service, barely having to think for myself. I just did my job, picked up my wages and it was so simple. I had not made any firm plans for civilian life as I was half expecting that I would decide to extend my RAF career. But shortly before I was due to leave the service something happened to change the course of my life.

During my year at RAF Valley I did a lot of singing as a solo artiste around the pubs and clubs all over Anglesey. The Wylfa Nuclear Power Station, near Cemaes Bay on the northern coast of the island, was in the course of being constructed with hundreds of construction workers on site. There was a social club for these workers on site and I managed to obtain a nice contract to sing at the Wylfa Power Station Social Club every Sunday evening. The club was up a long drive just outside the gates of the station. It had a large lounge bar and a sizeable concert room which had a capacity of about 150 people. The club used to get packed on a weekend. One particular Sunday

I was driving up to the club to do my show when I was met at the end of the drive by the chairman of the club, Mr Ivan Galley, who stopped me and gave me an envelope, he said, 'Tony, here's your fee, but you can turn around and go home because we won't be needing you tonight!' I asked him, 'Why ever not?' and he explained.

There had been a Saturday night dance at the club on the previous evening and at the end of the night, after everyone had gone home, the club steward decided to do a runner. He took with him all the money from the tills in the lounge bar and the concert room bar, plus all of the ticket money from the dance, every sixpenny piece out of the two fruit machines (one-arm bandits), all the money and all the cigarettes out of two cigarette machines, every bottle of spirits out of the cellar but he did not finish there. Within three or four weeks the club got invoices from four catalogue companies for orders for hampers, each containing about a dozen bottles of assorted spirits which had been delivered to the club! So it was a proper job! Rumour has it that he had loaded up all of this stuff and headed for the Isle of Man. To the best of my knowledge he was never found. On hearing this I decided I should be a bit opportunistic. I said to Ivan, 'I suppose you'll be looking for a new club steward.' He said that they would be, and as I was due to leave the RAF just three weeks later I asked Ivan to put my name forward for an interview for the job of club steward.

Wylfa Social Club was owned by four of the construction firms building the power station – English Electric, Taylor Woodrow, Babcock & Wilcox and Darchems. Each of the firms had representatives on the committee of the club. They gave me an interview at the end of which they told me straight away that they would like to offer me the job, and I gladly accepted the offer. So one week after leaving the Royal Air Force I started work as club steward of Wylfa Power Station Club. On my contract it said, 'with wife to assist!' Another new stage in my life was about to unfold.

The licensed trade was completely new to us, but we soon learned; anything we did not know we would pick up as we went along. Our first priority was to find somewhere to live. We applied for a council house, and because I was a recently demobbed serviceman we were put near the top of the list. To tide us over until we got a house we bought a twenty-two foot caravan and put it at the rear of the club with permission to connect up to the club's water and electricity supplies. This arrangement suited us fine for the two months we waited for our council house, which was in the neighbouring town of Amlwch, about seven miles from my work. Keeping the Wylfa Club was a new and great experience for Jean and me. We had a couple of barmaids to help so I was still able to do my Sunday evenings on stage. We had dances every other Saturday and the club was very well supported. The club was sponsored by the St Helens based Greenall Whitley Brewery through their local depot in Llanfairfechan, just outside Bangor, from where we received all our supplies of beer, spirits and cigarettes. The club committee arranged for the brewery to supply their own independent auditor, a Mr Fox, to come to the club and do a stocktake every month. No one could blame them for this after their experience with the previous steward.

Jean and I settled in to licensed trade very quickly and very well. Our customers were hard working men from all over the country who were good construction workers and were well paid. They were good drinkers and there was not a sign of trouble. Many had their wives staying with them in the area for the duration of their contract. For Jean and me it was a good introduction into the licensed trade and even though it was hard work we loved it. Every Sunday night I would entertain to a packed house in the concert room, while Jean and the two barmaids looked after the bars.

I had been at the club for about a year when the stocktaker, who was from Greenall Whitley's head office, told me that one of their pubs in Amlwch was shortly to become available, and that the brewery would like to know if we would be interested in taking it on. The thought of having our own pub quite excited us, and the idea of being our own boss and having the chance to develop a business on our own behalf was very attractive. Add to this the fact that the Wylfa Social Club where we were working only had a life of another year or two. Construction of the power station was nearing completion. The new power station was due to open and to go on stream for the CEGB (Central Electricity Generating Board) in 1971. So by then there would be no need of a club for the construction teams as CEGB had a big new club for the permanent staff, the opening of which was planned to coincide with the opening of the station.

Jean and I gave the brewery's proposition a lot of thought. We consulted a lot of people and I arranged an appointment with our bank manager to discuss it. He was very positive and thought it could be a good move for us, especially as we had been so successful and were so well thought of at Wylfa. This gave us a bit more confidence. So in 1969 I gave my notice in to Wylfa Social Club, accepted the brewery's offer and became the tenant and proud licensee of The Clock Inn, Amlwch with my name on a plaque above the front door.

I was now mine host of a small but very busy little local pub with a public bar on one side, and a comfortable lounge the other side with a serving area in between so we could serve both sides from the same central bar. Our living accommodation was upstairs on the first floor - quite small, but with a good sized lounge, a main bedroom, a small bedroom which Lynne and Mark shared and of course the kitchen and bathroom. We were within walking distance of the children's school. It suited us really well.

The pub was located in a terrace on the road down to Amlwch Port very near the centre of the town. We had a butcher's shop next door which had a sign in the window, 'Pleased to meet you – with meat to please you!' I always remember that sign. Why is it that you remember silly things like that?

I used to sing two or three nights a week in the pub. This was a sensible move for a good economic reason. To book an artiste would have cost me £8 or £10 at the time, while a barmaid for the evening would cost me £3 or £4. So it made sense! The Clock quickly became known as a music pub, and we did great business. Apart from singing myself there were a number of my locals who used to love to get up and give a song. They became regulars and brought along their supporters. It gave the evenings a good party feel.

I was singing in the pub one Friday evening when two couples came in for a drink. They sat down close to where I was set up, and when I had a break I sat down next to them and we had a chat. They were from Liverpool, and they had a holiday caravan down at a village called Llanelian, right on the coast a couple of miles outside Amlwch. Nice people. Our brewery, Greenall Whitley, had just brought out a new product, Grunhalle Lager. With my first order we got a couple of complimentary cases of pint glass tankards with the Grunhalle logo on, and two cases of similar half-pint glass tankards. One of the Liverpool ladies was drinking a half-pint of the lager from one of these tankards, and at the end of the evening I could see she was admiring it. It was obvious she wanted to slip it into her bag and take it home. She saw me looking and I nodded to her as if to say, 'Go on; put it in your bag.' So she went ahead obviously thinking that I was the hired singer.

The two couples were in town the following lunchtime on the Saturday, and they called in for a drink. I was now behind the bar. The one lady said, 'Are you the landlord?' I nodded. Bless her, she looked as if she wanted the ground to open and swallow her up. We had a good laugh about it afterwards, and they soon became great family friends, but I will never forget the look on her face when I confirmed I was the landlord of the pub. They really did become good friends; after we left the pub they invited Jean and me and the children to spend Christmas with them one year at their home in Liverpool. They made us most welcome, even taking me to see Everton at home on Boxing Day.

I used to take Wednesday evenings off. It may seem like a very strange reason – I used to entertain in another hotel in Amlwch – The Maesllwyn Hotel, otherwise known as The Trees. It was located on the edge of town, close to where we lived before moving into The Clock Inn. Jean looked after the pub for the evening and allowed me to go out and indulge myself in something different.

As I have been involved in country music for the past forty years people who have known me during that time often think that I must appreciate country music to the exclusion of every other kind of music. They could not be more wrong. I am a very keen fan of traditional jazz, particularly Chris Barber and Ken Colyer and their bands, and I have a real love of soul music. These days they call it 'Northern Soul' but to me it always was just soul music. Every Wednesday in the function room of The Trees I used to have a 'Soul Disco and Light Show'. I had hundreds of soul singles - everything from James Brown to all the Tamla Motown stars plus Otis Redding, Ray Charles, Aretha Franklin, Junior Walker and the All Stars and many more. Probably my very favourite record of any type of music (including country!) is a fantastic soul classic which I have loved ever since it was released in 1972 – *Love Train* by The O'Jays. I used to look forward to my Wednesday evenings as it was something totally different to anything else I did. I had a great crowd of enthusiastic followers and it was huge fun, and on a Wednesday evening The Trees was just bouncing!

We had been in The Clock Inn for a couple of years when we saw a problem developing. Our two children Lynne and Mark were sharing a bedroom, and Lynne was now twelve years old; the time was coming when she would need a room of her own. Some years previously the brewery had purchased the little two up, two down house next door with a view to extending the pub, and our living accommodation. However they did not allocate the necessary funds for the extension, which was very disappointing. They said it was likely to be three or four years before we could expect the alterations to be done, and so the time came that we told them we would have to move on. I did not know what we would move on to, but we would not starve. If the worst came to the worst I could always sing for my supper in the local pubs and clubs which I already had some experience of. I also might get a few bookings for my soul disco.

Greenall Whitley pulled out all the stops to keep us in one of their pubs. They offered us about fifteen pubs all over North Wales, but none of them were suitable. In most cases they were in 100% Welsh speaking areas so the schools' lessons were all in the Welsh language and this would have made things very difficult for the children, who only had a smattering of Welsh. As we could not find another pub that suited our needs we reluctantly had to terminate our contract with the brewery. We left The Clock Inn after a very happy two and a half years to move in another, unknown, direction.

CHAPTER 9

Melody Lane

When we left the pub we immediately applied for another council house, whilst as a short term measure we rented a little bungalow in Amlwch. We were very lucky because within a month we got our council house – six doors away from our previous house on the Maesllwyn Estate in Amlwch, very close to Lynne's school.

We decided that we enjoyed working for ourselves so much that instead of my looking for a job we would invest in ourselves. We managed to rent some shop premises right in the centre of Amlwch, and within a few weeks we had opened a music shop selling records and musical instruments and accessories: guitar strings etc. The shop was well stocked with LP's and singles including all the chart hits plus guitars, record players, amplifiers, accessories etc. We called the shop 'Melody Lane', and it became a meeting place for local musicians. I remember the very first delivery of records I received at the shop. The singles arrived including the No.1 hit of the day – *Chirpy Chirpy Cheep Cheep* by Middle of the Road.

My favourite story about our time in Melody Lane was when a young local lad came in and wanted to buy a guitar on hire purchase. This was no problem. The lad's name was Arfon Jones and he asked me if I would help him fill in the hire purchase agreement form. I got the form ready and asked him his full name – 'Arfon Jones.' I asked his address. He gave me that. I asked him, 'and what is your occupation, Arfon?' Arfon paused, and then replied, 'chicken catcher!' I said, 'what?!' he repeated, 'chicken catcher.' I couldn't believe this. All kinds of images were going through my mind. I asked him to explain. He said, 'I work for J.P. Woods (Chukie Chickens), the frozen chicken factory, and the wrapped frozen chickens come down a conveyer belt. I stand at the end of that conveyer belt, and catch the chickens off the end of it and put them in boxes of six! So those of us who do that are called chicken catchers.' I should have known!

At the same time as I opened the shop I started another business, a small entertainment agency serving many venues on the island of Anglesey, into Caernarfonshire and along the North Wales coast up to Llandudno and Rhyl. The agency was based in the back office of the music shop.

We only kept the shop for about ten months. It turned out that Amlwch was too small a town to make a specialist music shop viable; there were several bigger music and record stores to attract customers just a short drive or bus ride away in Holyhead or Bangor. So our shop was a bit of a financial disaster and we decided to cut our losses and give it up. The agency was working quite well though that too was not a great money spinner. But I was playing quite a lot, both as a solo artiste and with a four-piece band which I had formed with three friends. The band was called Midnight Sun, and we worked many social clubs on the island and across North Wales, including a number of holiday venues like hotels and caravan park clubs. One member of the band was a great pal of mine, Gordon Humphreys from Cemaes Bay on bass guitar, who had introduced me to the game of golf. Gordon and I spent many happy hours together on the course at Bull Bay Golf Club, which was in a lovely position on a headland overlooking the bay, just outside Amlwch. Gordon was an excellent golfer with a single figure handicap. I was a rank amateur and he used to give me a stroke a hole and still beat me, but it was still good fun. Also in the band we had two lads from Holyhead, Keith Hughes on drums and another who became a great friend, ace guitarist Eric Hughes on lead guitar and vocals. Eric and I did all the singing, and Eric also did a few instrumentals on guitar. We played a wide range of music right across the spectrum including chart hits, a bit of country music, rock and roll, in fact anything that people wanted. Up to this point I had never included any comedy on stage. I always loved jokes and off stage I had a million of them but never told them to an audience.

The first time I did give it a go was one evening when Midnight Sun were playing at the Snowdonia Country Club, Penisarwaun near Caernarfon. In a break between songs bass player Gordon said to me, 'Tell them a gag.' I thought, 'why not?' We had a good and lively audience so I tried one, and then another – and another! The audience loved it and were really responsive, and that was the start of things. Forever after that I always included an element of comedy whenever I appeared on stage. Midnight Sun became one of the busiest club bands in the area, playing clubs in Bangor like the Railway, Conservative and RAFA Clubs, Holyhead Conservative, British Legion and Royal Naval Clubs, Caernarfon Conservative, British Legion, Marbryn and Football Clubs, and various social clubs in Port Dinorwic, Llandudno, Penmaenmawr, Llanfairfechan and Rhyl.

We had regular bookings at a very nice caravan park on the island, Rynys Park Club, Dulas between Amlwch and Menai Bridge. This was the only club where we were ever asked to do an audition. We gladly agreed because the owner of the caravan park and club, Mr Roe, had a lot of work to offer. We turned up one afternoon, brought our equipment in, and set up. Our audience was Mr Roe who sat on his own in the middle of the dance floor! We had half a dozen songs ready to sing for him. We started the first song, a Herman's Hermits song *Something is Happening*. We got half way through the song when he stopped us, told us to pack our gear away and come into his office. We loaded the gear into the cars, and when we reached his office he gave us about sixty gigs spread over the next twelve months and he gave us a lot of support. A very nice man! We also did a lot of work at the Star Motel, LlanfairPG, you know, the place with the long name. (I can say it if you want!) They used to book a lot of star cabaret acts, and we played for dancing as a support act to the star names.

I recall one time doing a solo booking at a lovely little club on another caravan park. This one was at Red Wharf Bay on the east coast of Anglesey. I sang all my usual stuff and in my break a couple of holiday makers approached me at the bar and said, 'You seem to do quite a bit of country music. Can you do any more?' I had a list of about three hundred songs which I had found were popular. I showed it to them and they said, 'Oh yes. There's a lot of country on this list. Would you be able to do a whole evening of country music?' I told them that if the material on that list was suitable then it would be no problem. I used to sing stuff by Glen Campbell, Johnny Cash, Jim Reeves, George Jones, John Denver, Marty Robbins, George Hamilton IV and Charlie Pride among others. The couple were called Terry and Maureen Barker, and they told me that they were the organisers of a specialist country music club near Stoke-on-Trent and if I was prepared to travel that far they would give me a booking. I replied, 'If the money is right, I'll travel anywhere!'

They offered me a good fee and booked me to play at the Keep it Country Club which was held at the Conservative Club, Newcastle-under-Lyme near Stoke. I had never even heard of a country music club at the time and it was all new to me, but they happily accepted all the material I did. A few years later I was invited back to play several times, but this booking was my very first experience of a country music club. I was singing my heart out to an attentive listening audience, and I loved it.

My agency work was going very well, it kept me busy in the daytime, and I could still go out singing at night. Once in January I received a call from the Plas-y-Bryn Hotel in the hills of Snowdonia outside Caernarfon. A new owner had taken over the place, a Mr Alan Frost from the Birmingham area who had sold his wholesale greengrocery business and bought this lovely hotel. He told me he wanted to put star cabaret on four nights a week through the summer season in his function room, which he was turning into a French Restaurant, complete with Michelin Star Chef. Could I help him with his entertainment programme? This was a phone call from heaven for any agency!

I drove over to meet up with him and he told me what he would need. He wanted a backing trio of musicians who could read music to back the stars and to play for dancing at the end of the evening. He also wanted star names who people would know and he said he would accommodate them for the four days they were playing there. Could I help? I certainly could. I told him it would be no problem and when I got home I went to work on it straight away. There was an excellent trio who lived in Holyhead who were perfect for the backing and dancing job. The summer season was going to be ten weeks long so I needed ten names and I put together a programme which he readily accepted. The names who appeared there during that summer were Joe Brown, Susan Maughan, Julie Rogers, Ken Goodwin and George Roper, (both from TV's 'The Comedians'), ventriloquist Ray Alan and Lord Charles, David Whitfield and Joe 'Mr Piano' Henderson.

It was a great contract for me but unfortunately the contract turned out to be only for one season; the hotel was sold at the end of that year and Mr Frost the owner moved back to Birmingham. It was good while it lasted!

The agency covered all sorts of entertaining, including singers in clubs and pubs, and arranging work for many local artistes. I would also bring in cabaret artistes and speciality acts from Manchester and Liverpool to appear in clubs all over North Wales. By working in co-operation with agencies in Manchester, Merseyside and the Midlands I was able to offer the North Wales clubs everything they needed in the way of entertainment. It was, in the main, stage entertainment they wanted but I remember receiving a request from a large club on the coast, Llandudno Junction Labour Club, 'Could I provide them with an evening of professional wrestling?'

This was a new one for me! Professional wrestling was massive in the 60s and 70s. It was televised every Saturday afternoon for about an hour on ITV's World of Sport, introduced by Dickie Davies with commentary by Kent Walton. The wrestling was on for an hour just before the football results. It was a prime slot on TV and it became hugely popular, the top stars becoming household names. I managed to get the phone number of one of the biggest names in the sport. He was Jackie 'Mr TV' Pallo, and he had a company called 'Jackie Pallo Enterprises,' which promoted wrestling evenings at theatres and clubs all over the country. I phoned him and obtained all the details and prices etc. and went back to the Junction Labour Club with a package. The package featured four bouts of wrestling, including some names from TV, and starring Jackie himself and his son, Jackie Pallo Junior. The club committee were thrilled with what was on offer so I booked it for them, and the evening was a terrific success. This was the first of many such evenings of professional wrestling I arranged for clubs all over North Wales in conjunction with Jackie Pallo Enterprises and other promoters.

We featured the top TV names of the time including, of course, Jackie Pallo and Son, Les Kellett, The Royals (Bert Royal and his brother, Vic Faulkner,) Mick McMichael, Kendo Nagasaki, Billy Two Rivers, Adrian Street and many more. For a couple of years it became a big part of my agency work.

My close association with agencies in Manchester and Liverpool gave me access to artistes and club entertainers who had never been seen before in North Wales. I booked top TV comedians many of whom had been seen on Granada TV's 'The Comedians,' including George Roper, Colin Crompton, Duggie Brown, Frank Carson, Lee Wilson and Ken Goodwin. Female impersonators or 'drag acts' as they were known were very popular with our clubs. Manchester was a hotbed of these speciality acts. Artistes like Billy 'Pet' Clarke, Billy and Bobbie Steele, Misster Lennie Mortan and Diamonds Lamour were regular visitors to our area and became very popular in our clubs.

I could not leave this area of my work without mentioning the artiste whom I consider to be the most talented I have ever worked with. That was the simply amazing Irish singer, comedian and impressionist Danny Fontana. Danny was based in Manchester for a short while in the seventies, and I was fortunate enough to book him for several shows in North Wales with his backing band, the five piece Birds and Bees, three boys and two girls who were a wonderful harmony band and multi-talented musicians.

Danny was unique. Whether he was singing a monster ballad like *The Impossible Dream*, or taking off Elvis with *A Fool Such As I*, or performing one of his hilarious comedy routines he was brilliant, and everything that I aspired to be on stage. The close of his show meant a standing ovation every time. Seeing him on stage so many times influenced me and my work tremendously. The Birds and Bees, who were based in Dublin, were immensely talented and their special version of the unaccompanied Neil Young classic *After the Goldrush*, was a showstopper. This song *After the Goldrush* was covered and taken into the Top 20 in this country by a band called Prelude, now known as American Routes on the British country scene. Their version also went to No.1 in Canada and Australia and No.12 in the USA.

Danny Fontana and the Birds and Bees impressed me so much that later, when I moved to Shrewsbury, I even booked them to come to Shropshire to do a few shows.

But my agency work was only a stop-gap. I did not really want to spend my life in an office booking artistes and shows for other people. It had helped me to keep the wolf from the door for a while, but I had other ideas of what I wanted to do with my life.

After the demise of Melody Lane Jean and I sat down together and had a long discussion. I said that what I would really like to do is have a shot at becoming a full time professional entertainer. To be quite honest, although we loved Anglesey, and we were very settled there, we knew it was not the right place to be based as an entertainer. In order to travel the country, as I hoped to do, I needed to be much more central instead of out on a limb in the top corner of North Wales. It was a three hour drive on bad roads to get anywhere near an area where I would be able to get enough work. It was going to be a big decision to leave a place which we loved and where we really had put down roots, to venture into the unknown and to try something which we were not sure would succeed for us. But after much heart searching we took the decision and it was probably the best decision we have ever made.

CHAPTER 10

A New Beginning

This move was going to be another new beginning for us. We were going to have to start from scratch again. After our life in the RAF and a period in the licensed trade we seemed to have just plodded along with no real sense of purpose. This really was a step into the unknown. There is a wealth of difference between doing a few gigs as a semi-pro artiste or band member, and becoming a full time professional. Being a professional artiste means that you have to work to pay your rent, feed the family, and cover all the usual weekly, monthly and annual outgoings which every family has. But you don't have a pay packet to collect at the end of the week! It was a gamble alright, but we felt it was an educated gamble. I was coming up to forty years old at the time and I thought to myself, and I said to Jean, 'I really want to try this because if I don't have a shot at it now I'll never do it, and if that happens I will probably regret it for the rest of my life.'

I decided I would need a stage name. My real name was far too ordinary to have on a billboard outside the London Palladium! I remember exactly how and when I chose the name 'Tony Best.' One Saturday night our band Midnight Sun were playing at the cricket club in Bangor, and there was a large poster on the wall at the side of the stage advertising the names of the bands for the next four Saturdays. The poster was divided into four horizontal slots. At the top was tonight's band, ourselves – Midnight Sun in medium sized lettering. The next week it was to be a band called Exodus – in great big letters. The following band was The League of Gentlemen – in very small lettering because of the number of letters in their name. Finally it was a band called The Naturals – like ourselves, medium sized lettering.

Straight away I thought to myself: my stage name has to be as short as possible to make sure it stands out on posters. I felt I should keep the first name Tony and I decided on a four letter surname to keep it even. You can never get better than 'Best' so that was what I decided upon. Job done!

To be a professional artiste based right out on a limb in Anglesey would have been very difficult. We were ninety miles from Liverpool, 120 miles from Manchester and 150 miles from Birmingham, and the roads were not good. When we visited Jean's family in Shropshire it was always a three hour drive down the old A5. There was not enough work available in North Wales to make it viable as a full time artiste and we decided we would have to move house to somewhere more central.

Jean is a Shropshire girl so Shropshire seemed to be the ideal place to base ourselves. It is in the middle of the country. Jean's Mum and Dad plus two of her three sisters and all four of her brothers lived in the county. Jean had spent the first twenty years of her life there so it was familiar territory, and we would not be alone in a strange place.

We were living in a three bedroom council house in Anglesey and we found out that it was possible to exchange houses if we were able to find a willing party in another part of the country. We placed an advert in the *Shropshire Star*, the county's daily newspaper, offering an exchange. Unbelievably within just two days we had a reply. A chap who lived with his family in Bayston Hill, Shrewsbury, but was originally from Anglesey, had just secured a job at Ysbyty Gwynedd, the hospital in Bangor. He was looking to move up to Bangor or Anglesey as soon as possible. We invited him to come up and see our house. He came the very next day with his wife, and they said it would be perfect for them. We drove down to Shrewsbury to view his house, which was fine for us. So the deal was done, and within two weeks we had moved to Bayston Hill to start this new chapter in our lives. We even shared a removals van, a Shrewsbury based firm bringing their stuff up to Anglesey, and unloading it, before loading our furniture and taking it to Shrewsbury for us. It was all done the same day.

The sheer speed at which this move took place was not quite how I had envisaged things happening. I had no work in the new area. I still had a few gigs in the diary in North Wales, but we had a little savings which we thought we may have to dip into until I sorted out some work for myself. To be honest, the following two years were financially by far the most difficult times that we had ever encountered, and we certainly struggled.

When we arrived in Shrewsbury, apart from Jean's family, we only knew one other person in the area. This was a comedian, Danny Dalton (real name Kevin Dalton), whom I used to book through my agency in Anglesey for clubs along the North Wales coast. I contacted Kevin when we arrived, and he was kind enough to introduce me to a number of pubs and clubs in the area which put entertainment on and for this I was very grateful.

Every Wednesday I would drive seventy-five miles up the A5 to Llanberis to sing at the Dolbadarn Hotel for a fee of £40. Fortunately petrol was about 70p a gallon so I spent about £4 on petrol and the rest was a start to my week's income. There were a few other bookings up in North Wales in those early days which helped. Jean got herself a job working in the cafeteria of the Littlewoods Store in the middle of Shrewsbury so her wages went into the kitty as well.

I was completely unknown in the area (or anywhere really!) so I immediately set to work to rectify this. The first thing I did was to obtain the addresses of as many entertainment agencies as I could lay my hands on. Initially I concentrated on the local area, and then further afield. Then I put together a promotional pack with a few photos, a short biography, and a run down on the sort of thing I did. I sent this pack to all the agents on my list with an offer to audition or to do a showcase spot for them. This effort got a limited response, but I did get a bit of work from it so it was a start. Next I visited the town's public library and looked at all the entertainment pages of the *Shropshire Star* for the previous couple of months. I made a list of any venue, pub or club which advertised entertainment. Then I sat down with the phone and got to work ringing them all. It felt like begging!

The pitch went something like this – 'Hello, my name is Tony Best. I'm an entertainer and I'm new in the area. I sing and play piano accordion, and try to get the audience involved. I wondered if you might like to give me a trial booking.' They usually came back with, 'Well, how much do you charge?' And I would say, 'However much you're prepared to pay me for the first time in!' It is very difficult trying to sell yourself without sounding big headed. You cannot say, 'Look, you've got to book me because I'm brilliant!' I managed to get a few bookings to put in the diary. But I did have one great piece of luck.

One of my phone calls was to The New Inn in the village of Prees, near Whitchurch. The landlord was a Mr Stan Pritchard. We got to the bit where he asked, 'How much do you charge?' I said that I did not know, and he said, 'Well, I put entertainment on three evenings a week and I pay all the others £16, will that be OK?' I said it would be fine and he replied that he had a Friday night available three weeks later. He booked me for the date and I looked forward to it. When that Friday came along there was a good crowd in the pub and we had a really good night, after which I packed my gear away and loaded it in the car. Stan said, 'Come into the back room and I'll get your money.' He gave me £18 and said, 'There's a bit extra there as you gave us a great night.' He went on to say, 'It must be hard trying to get bookings when nobody has ever heard of you.' I said that it was. He said, 'Well if you ever phone anyone and they want a recommendation, just tell them to phone me.' I took that offer up, and everyone I rang seemed to know him. I got quite a bit of work as a result of his offer, and I played regularly at The New Inn after that. The going rate around the pubs in Telford, Shrewsbury, Oswestry and around the villages was about £16 a night. Sometimes a bit more and sometimes a bit less, but I just took anything that was offered just to fill the diary.

The first pub I ever played at in the local area was in the village of Pontesbury, about eight miles outside Shrewsbury. It was only a small pub and in the lounge bar there was a space where the artiste set up. They would close the shutters on the dartboard and the artiste would set up in front of the dartboard. I put a speaker on the juke box which was on one side and the other speaker on the fruit machine which was on the other side. There was an open area in front of me and seating to the back and to both sides. The pub was packed and I started singing and all the time I sang there were four or five chaps standing about four feet from me blocking my view of the audience, and who did not stop chatting to each other all night, taking no notice of me. I pressed on and just did my spots, thinking to myself, 'I'm not enjoying this one bit! If I didn't really need this fifteen quid I'd be out of here like a shot.'

I carried on and at the end of the evening I packed my gear away and went over to the landlady at the bar who gave me my £15. She then said, 'Now, when can we have you again?' I said, 'You've got to be joking. They never took any notice of me all night.' 'Oh,' she said, 'They liked you!' I said, 'How do you make that out?' 'Look,' she said, 'There are three other pubs in this village. If they don't enjoy someone, this place empties and they all go down the road. You kept them in! Now, when can you come back?' I said, 'I'll give you a ring!' I think I must have forgotten.

With the help of my phone calls and Stan's recommendations a few bookings came in and we struggled on through 1975 into the start of the following year. I got a bit of work through a couple of agencies, Cambrian Entertainments based in mid Wales and Bernie and Pat Lewis of Kama Entertainment Agency based in Much Wenlock, Shropshire, but it really was hard going.

To help us get through this rough period I answered an advert for part time work in a William Hill Betting Office in the middle of Shrewsbury. I got the job and worked a few afternoons a week settling bets. After about three or four weeks the area manager asked me if I would be interested in taking a four week management course in Leeds. The company provided accommodation for the four weeks and I would be home at weekends. I decided that as my singing career was not exactly rocketing I would give it a go.

There were about twenty of us on the course from various parts of the country. We were all accommodated in The Clock Hotel (coincidentally!) in Roundhay Road, Leeds and our classroom was in the City Centre. It was quite a pleasant four weeks. I found the work interesting but not stretching and passed the exams at the end of the course without too much trouble. Shortly afterwards I was contacted by head office, and offered the post of manager at William Hill's High Street office in Shrewsbury. I accepted the job and suddenly I found that I actually had a proper job.

This meant I had a regular wage coming in and I was still able to go out singing in the evenings. At the end of each day's racing I had to make sure the books were balanced, lock up the office and deposit the day's takings in the night safe of the bank which was about fifty yards away from my office. There was no evening racing in those days so I was always finished by about 6pm.

We had been living in Shrewsbury about eight months when I took on the post of betting office manager. It had been a very difficult time but the job gave us a bit of a financial cushion in our week to week expenses. It was only a stop-gap move, but it gave me an added incentive to put more effort into getting established on the entertainment scene. I was certainly getting better known on the local pub and club scene. Of course because of the day job, I could not take work that was any distance away so I was limited to a maximum travelling distance of about forty miles away from Shrewsbury at the very most. But this did not cause any difficulties at first. I was able to get plenty of gigs close to hand in Shrewsbury and the surrounding villages.

My childhood home - "The Laurels," East Aberthaw

The famous 14th century pub in my home village,
East Aberthaw "THE BLUE ANCHOR."

A couple of photos of my Mum and Dad.

Mum and me.

Me and my big sister, Peggy.

RAF Locking 1st XI 1955/1956
Brian Prole, Sarge Searle, Smudge Smith, Derek Taylor, Maurice Geary,
Eric Ellis, Taff Southern, Taff Evans, Bob Browning, Rick Harris, Taff Jarrett

RAF Locking 1st XI
Extreme left standing.

22nd March 1958
Jean and me on our big day.

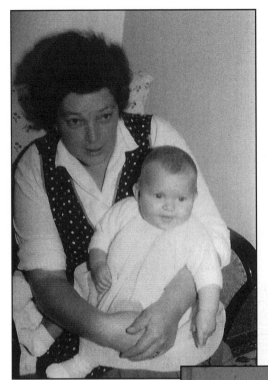

Our next door neighbour in Germany, "our guardian angel," Helen Wallace with our baby, Lynne in 1959.

Jean and me at a night out at the Families Club, Goch, winning a spot prize at the dance.

A couple of photos of my band in Germany 1959/1960.
"THE TRAMPS"

Singing at the Greyhound, Sutton Bridge in 1963 with
One of my RAF mates from work, "Shaky" Pitt.

Lynne and Mark

CHAPTER 11

It's Getting Better!

As a few months went by I was still singing in the local pubs, but I was playing more and more in social clubs and sports clubs where the work was a bit better and it was a bit better paid. This was fine, but occasionally you are fortunate enough to get a lucky break. My lucky break happened in September 1976. I was contacted by a man who had seen me perform in a local hotel and on the strength of that he offered me a great contract. His name was Ken Smith, and he owned a sixteenth century Inn – The Bear at Hodnet, near Market Drayton. The Bear was noted for its weekly medieval banquets and he was looking for someone to be his new Court Jester. The job involved a bit of singing but mostly running the evening, and making sure the audience got involved in the evening's activities. He told me he thought the job would suit me perfectly, and when he described just what was needed I thought it was right up my street.

He offered me the job for the whole of the following year, 1977. The banquets were held every Friday and Saturday throughout the year and every single night in December, plus a special festive banquet at lunchtime on Christmas Day. This made a total of over 120 bookings in the year. My ship had come in! My fee was to be £35 per night. He invited Jean and me to attend one of the current banquets to give me an idea of just what was going to be needed of me. The evening consisted of a staggering seven-course meal, eaten with the fingers and no knives and forks. There would be an opening spot from me at the start of the evening and during the meal, and there would be a couple of cabaret spots from a speciality act, The Great Hanleo, who did a knife-throwing and fire-eating act as well as working with a huge python. There was also a DJ to play for dancing at the end of the evening. I was delighted to accept his offer and I looked forward to starting the job in the January.

These banquets had been taking place at The Bear Inn for a couple of years, and Mr Smith had decided that they needed a bit of a change in format and an injection of excitement. I obviously had some preparations to make. I wrote an exciting new script for the running story of the banquet and got his approval. The Baron and Baroness were at the top table, on the stage, and during the course of the evening messages kept coming through that the Black Knight was getting nearer and nearer to our castle to kidnap the Baroness and have his wicked way with her! The Black Knight was none other than Gerard Naprous the famed horseman, stunt horse trainer and stunt co-ordinator for television and film who had his stables in mid Wales. When the Black Knight arrived at the castle he would come up the stairs to the Baronial Hall with a huge white stallion, which he mounted, galloped the length of the room between the tables and reared up before being confronted by the White Knight, the DJ in disguise, who was going to defend the Baroness's honour. Then followed an excitingly choreographed sword fight in which the Black Knight was vanquished and the Baron and his lady, whose honour had been preserved, made their exit. Then it was time for the disco to round off a terrific evening's entertainment. This was a great contract for me and it came at just the right time.

Due to the restrictions which the day job put on me I was unable to travel far so I filled my diary with gigs around the local pubs and clubs. Later on in the year I got another very lucky break. I received a phone call for a first time booking at a country pub in Staffordshire, about thirty miles from home. It was The Duke of York at Mill Meece, a super village pub just outside Eccleshall. At the end of the evening on my first visit there the landlord, Roger, offered me a residency for every Tuesday evening and every Sunday lunchtime for the following twelve months. My diary was clear on Tuesday evenings and on Sunday lunchtimes so I was pleased to take the gigs with no hesitation.

This was in late 1976, the UK national average wage for a forty-four hour working week was just under £80.00, and this contract meant that with the two nights at The Duke of York, and the two nights a week medieval banquets at The Bear I was well ahead of this figure. With the two residencies it still left me four nights a week for any other bookings, and it meant that I was now in a position to quit my day job with William Hill. I could finally concentrate full time on filling my diary with the work I enjoyed the most - my entertaining. We had a very successful year doing the medieval banquets and playing at 'The Duke', and at the end of the year my contract for the banquets was extended for a second year at an increased fee, and so was my residency at The Duke of York.

It had been a very hard time for the Best family during those early days in Shrewsbury, and we really struggled. Starting from scratch in an area where no one had ever heard of me was a lot more difficult than I imagined it would be. I was so grateful for the help of people like Stan Pritchard at The New Inn at Prees for offering me references for other prospective bookers, and of my only contact in Shrewsbury, my friend Kevin Dalton for his support and introductions to venues where I might get a booking. However the turning point was definitely the call from Ken Smith at The Bear, and his booking of me for the medieval banquets. Things really looked up after that.

We really loved living in Shropshire, and we have ever since. Jean loved it of course because she was living close to her family for the first time since marrying me, and being carted off away from them to Germany and Anglesey! I loved it for the simple reason that I was now doing what I would have liked to be doing twenty years previously. So life seemed definitely to be on the up and up; things had started to move. I handed in my notice to William Hill Ltd. and left the day job. Jean also quit her job at Littlewoods Store Cafeteria, and that left her free so that she could travel with me if I went any distance. I was now able to travel further afield with my music should I get the opportunity - and the opportunities soon started to arrive including many from entertainment agencies.

I was on the books of several specialist country music agencies and this brought in quite a bit of work which I would never have got if left to my own devices. To pick up contacts and to take your bookings direct with a venue is always advantageous because there is no commission to pay, and the whole of your fee is your own. However I never begrudged an agency who had given me a booking their commission; these agencies were able to introduce me to new venues and even new areas of the country. So I made it my policy to send an agent's commission the very next day. After all that bit of the fee did not belong to me anyway. Agencies I worked for included the Mike and Margaret Storey Agency of Huddersfield in Yorkshire, Allen Promotions run by Lee Williams of Wantage in Oxfordshire, and the Drew Taylor Agency of Biggar in Scotland. For local work I was also on the books of the Kama Agency of Bernie and Pat Lewis of Much Wenlock in Shropshire and Michael Davies's Cambrian Entertainments in Trefeglwys in mid Wales. I had very good relationships with them all, and I appreciated what they did for me.

Two or three years previously when we made the decision for me to go full time, and for us to up sticks and move house to be more central for the new career we knew it was not going to be easy. The lightning speed with which we made the move from Anglesey to Shrewsbury compounded the problem; I had not had time to prepare the ground in my new area so we struggled. But now it was very gratifying to see things coming together for us. The contracts for the banquets and for The Duke of York were most important starting blocks, and the other work starting to come in regularly was a welcome bonus.

For the first time since the move we came to the conclusion that we might have done the right thing!

CHAPTER 12

The Pubs and Clubs

After giving up the full time day job with William Hill Ltd. I was now available to travel anywhere without getting back for work the next morning. But for the following couple of years the vast majority of my work was still in the pubs and clubs in Shropshire with occasional gigs in the neighbouring counties of Staffordshire, Herefordshire, Cheshire, also West Midlands, mid Wales and North Wales.

For the first couple of months after giving up the job I devoted my time to the telephone, ringing venues I had previously been unable to take bookings for. I had already got a really good start to each week's wages with my residencies at the medieval banquets at The Bear, and of course my Tuesday evenings and Sunday lunchtimes at The Duke of York. However I still needed to fill the diary with two or three other evenings each week.

I was quite amazed at the number of village pubs in Shropshire who put on regular entertainment on weekday nights. These were the venues I approached in an attempt to fill the spaces in my diary for the next few months. Fortunately over the previous eighteen months I had built up a decent reputation around the area, and so it wasn't too difficult. Looking back on my old diaries for that time I see that in 1977/78 I played over forty pubs in Shropshire alone, and another twenty-odd in the neighbouring counties.

I was happy doing the pubs and getting better known in the area, but as the months went by the quality of the work seemed to improve. I was getting more and more enquiries for private parties, sports and social clubs and even a few specialist country music venues. There were ten social clubs in Shrewsbury itself, another thirty in the rest of Shropshire and many more in mid Wales and around the Midlands. So there really was plenty of work available.

I remember being booked in August 1977 for a special evening at a pub about nine miles out of Shrewsbury near the village of Minsterley. It was The More Arms, and the special booking was for their Harvest Supper evening. They booked me to appear with a country singer who became a great friend later on. He was known as 'Britain's Mr Country Music', Tony Goodacre. We had a great night working together. The landlord of the pub was someone else with whom I struck up a good friendship. His name was Alvin Evans. Alvin had a long history of heart trouble, and he used to put on an occasional charity show in the local Minsterley Village Hall in aid of the Royal Shrewsbury Hospital's Coronary Care Unit. Alvin invited me to appear on one of these shows in the November - a country music special. He wanted me to do a spot and to compere the evening. I was delighted to accept and that invitation triggered off something very special.

The show featured three local country singers plus a well known country band from Bristol The Kelvin Henderson Band, the popular country singer Lee Montana and top of the bill were the brilliant international TV stars - Miki and Griff. What a night! And what a thrill for me to work with the amazing Miki and Griff. They were the epitome of professionalism; there were many young artistes who could have gone to one of their shows to see just how to conduct themselves on stage. They could learn how to take a bow and how to handle an audience; this couple were just superb. Bear in mind that this was a village hall out in the Shropshire countryside. There was no dressing room available at Minsterley Hall so Alvin had arranged for a small touring caravan to be placed just outside the stage door for Miki and Griff's use as a dressing room. Ten minutes before they were due on stage I knocked on the caravan door and went in. Griff was at the bathroom hand basin looking in the mirror and polishing his teeth. Now that is what you call professionalism!

During the interval in the show I was mingling with the audience and found myself in conversation with a group of country music enthusiasts including the late Ken Johnson, who was a traffic policeman in Shrewsbury, and Margaret Jones (now Murray) both of whom said that they felt it a great shame that there was so little good country music available in the Shropshire area. In fact Ken remarked, 'There's such a great following for it, someone should start a country music club in Shrewsbury.' I didn't give his remark much thought at the time, but a little while later I did.

I used to sing on some Sunday evenings in a small social club on the outskirts of town: the Seven Acres Club. It was owned by a local builder Mr Keith Davies of Owenward Contractors Ltd. I think the club was his hobby. Thinking back to Ken Johnson's remarks when we were at Minsterley Hall it set my mind going, and I came to the conclusion that it might be worth a try to start a country music club in Shrewsbury. I had never done anything like it before but the idea quite appealed to me. I checked all over Shropshire to see if there was any competition, and discovered that Ken was right: there were no country music clubs in the Shropshire area. In fact the nearest one was over thirty miles away at The Anchor, Kerry, near Newtown in mid Wales. Otherwise the nearest ones were in Worcester, Birmingham or Stoke all of which were about fifty miles away from Shrewsbury. Next I checked with my diary and noticed that I didn't have a single Monday booked in the following six months so if I was going to arrange something on a regular basis it would have to be on Mondays.

The next time I was playing at Seven Acres Club I had a chat with Keith Davies, the owner, and asked if he would mind me putting on a regular country music evening on Mondays at his club. Keith and his wife, Ethel, were most enthusiastic and extremely helpful. I settled on alternate Mondays for the club. Heaven knows where the name Lazyacre came from! It was just a name I thought of at the time.

It took me a couple of months to sort all the details out. Seven Acres Club was a very warm and welcoming venue with a capacity of about 120. I invited my friends Vince Layne and Bobby King (Layne and King), to be resident duo with me on all clubnights. I then booked a guest act of either a soloist, or a duo or a band for each show for the first three months. We were ready to be up and running for our first show at the beginning of March 1978. I had no expectation of the club running for more than a few months, or a year at the most, but I felt it was certainly worth a try.

I would open the show with a few songs followed by a spot from Layne and King, and then our guest artiste. After a break the second half of the show would be a longer spot from our guest artiste, at the end of which Layne and King and I would join the guest act for a grand finale when we did a couple of songs altogether. The format worked very well right from the start.

CHAPTER 13

Lazyacre – the Early Years

After a couple of months planning and a little advertising of the club's existence Lazyacre Country Music Club opened its doors for the club's first show on Monday 6th March 1978. Our guest artiste on this opening night was Welshman Dave Curtis, originally from Harlech, but now living locally, and who was somewhat of a local hero at the time. He had been a winner on the popular television talent show *New Faces*. Dave, an excellent singer and yodeller, was the perfect choice to star on Lazyacre's opening evening. We stuck to our planned running order with me opening the show with a few songs. The first song ever sung at Lazyacre was the Bob Wills classic *San Antonio Rose*. It was also the first track on side one of my very first album a little later. After Vince and Bobby had done a few numbers I introduced our guest artiste, Dave Curtis, who gave us a couple of great spots before Layne and King and I joined him for our grand finale. Lazyacre's first clubnight had gone very well and I was convinced it was going to be the start of greater things to come at the Lazyacre in the future. How right I was!

Membership of the club was set at £1 per year, and the cost of admission to shows was £1 or £1.25, up to £2 for special shows with star names. Attendance was one hundred on the first night and of these about seventy joined as full members of Lazyacre CMC. Within the first few months we had such names at the club as Britain's top country band The Hillsiders, those delightful TV stars Miki and Griff, The Karl Denver Trio, and top American bluegrass duo Bill Grant and Delia Bell. Bill and Delia were the club's very first visiting American artistes. We also featured local country bands like Brian Martin and the Marauders from Stoke-on-Trent and the brilliant Cotton Gin from Birmingham. By August the club's attendances had settled down to a consistent 120, and by the end of the year membership of the club totalled 275. Our clubnights were all in concert with no dance floor.

We did try leaving a floor space on one occasion early in the club's existence and invited dancers to use it, but everyone still just sat and listened so we scrubbed that idea. Lazyacre has been a concert club ever since. Our members seem to like it that way.

Of course I was still working the clubs and pubs, and I did a show one evening with my pals Layne and King at Biddulph Moor Village Hall near Stoke-on-Trent. One of the guests asked us if his young daughter could sing a couple of songs with her guitar during our interval. She was about fifteen years old. We fixed her up with a microphone, and when we had a break she got up and sang a few country songs and a little novelty comedy number. She was very nervous but very, very good, and she got a great reception. Her name was Carole Gordon.

At the end of the evening I spoke to her Dad and Mum and told them that if they would like to bring her over to Shrewsbury one Monday evening she could do a short spot at Lazyacre. They agreed to come over to our club, and the Monday they chose was in the November, they brought about forty friends and supporters in a coach. Our guest artistes on the night were Bob Newman and Slim Pickins. Carole did her short spot and once again did really well. At the end of the evening we all got together on stage for a few songs, Layne and King, Bob and Slim and myself, and we invited Carole to join us for this little jam session. Her harmony singing was just brilliant. Carole's short appearance that night was to have great significance later on.

When American bluegrass duo Bill Grant and Delia Bell appeared at Lazyacre it was as a part of their week long country and bluegrass tour of England, arranged by Midlands promoter Don Page. Bill and Delia were top of the bill and were backed by a band from Kent. Layne and King and I were invited by Don to be part of the tour. This was my first experience of what I called 'properly touring the country' as a professional entertainer so it was quite a milestone in my career. The short tour started with the show at Lazyacre followed by shows in Bloxwich near Walsall, Herne Bay in Kent, Ringwood in Hampshire, Bridgwater in Somerset and finishing off at Fry's Club, Keynsham, near Bristol. The whole tour was a great success and this new experience was most enjoyable for me personally.

Lazyacre's first Christmas show featured a terrific country band from Warrington, Poacher, closing a great first year for the club. At the end of the year our host club, Seven Acres Club, was sold by Keith Davies to Mr & Mrs Dennis Boyle owners of The Baron's Club in Wellington Centre. We were very sorry to lose Keith and Ethel Davies who had given us tremendous support in our first year. We hoped to have similar co-operation from the new owners.

The club's success continued through 1979. We opened the year's programme with a return visit to the club by Liverpool's Hillsiders who, at the time, were without equal as Britain's top country band, and we presented the five of them with their trophies as winners in Lazyacre's first awards. They had won the 'Most Popular Band' category, with the 'Most Popular Solo Artiste' award being won by Dave Curtis, and the 'Most Popular Duo' award being won by Slim Pickins & Bob Newman. Voting forms had been sent out to members with the club's Christmas newsletter.

Also with the start of the New Year we said farewell to Layne and King who had done a brilliant job as resident duo for the club's first nine months of operations. Vince and Bobby had decided to split up and to pursue solo careers, and everyone at Lazyacre wished them luck for the future. Bobby played and sang around the pubs and clubs in the Midlands, and Vince gained a great reputation with his stunning 'Tribute to Jim Reeves'.

We continued to have a very ambitious entertainment programme which featured many top British acts such as The Muskrats, Tex Withers, West Virginia, Tammy Cline, John Aston, Frank Jennings, Patsy Powell, Jeannie Denver, Pete Sayers, David H. Lee and Ken Harris. We also welcomed many international artistes including that superb American singer/songwriter Jimmy Payne, who is a personal favourite of mine, three sensational American fiddle players Tokyo Matsu, Shoji Tabuchi and Billy Armstrong, and two great acts from Canada, singer/songwriter, Dick Damron and the wonderful Family Brown.

Disappointingly by the end of the year we found we were not getting the co-operation we had hoped for from Seven Acres Club owners, Mr and Mrs Boyle, so we decided to move to a new venue. In January 1980 after twenty-two months at Seven Acres Club Lazyacre moved to our new home in the Regency Suite of The Lord Hill Hotel in Abbey Foregate, Shrewsbury. During the previous twenty-two months Lazyacre had grown from simply being what we thought was a good idea to being one of the best country music clubs in Great Britain. Our new venue could comfortably accommodate two hundred people as opposed to a maximum of 140 at the previous place.

The Lord Hill turned out to be an ideal venue for us, with the extra capacity enabling us to be even more ambitious in planning our future shows, and over the next few years at the club we saw names like Colorado, Tammy Cline, Lonnie Donegan, The Frank Jennings Syndicate, Patsy Powell and the Goodtimers, Ken Harris & the Playboys, Shag Connors' Carrot Crunchers, Bob McKinlay, Bert Weedon and Stu Stevens. We also had a number of international artistes like Canada's Gordie West, Kathy Stewart, Ralph Carlson's Country Mile, American singer/songwriters, Dick Feller and Steve Young, and the great Frank Ifield.

Miki and Griff returned to the club for our Second Anniversary Show and they accepted our invitation to become Honorary Presidents of Lazyacre. Miki and Griff took a great interest in the club as Honorary Presidents, and after Miki's sad death in 1989 Griff continued to keep in touch until he too sadly passed away in 1995. Miki and Griff were great troupers in the old music hall tradition, and were dedicated to country music. They were very proud to have been the first British act ever to appear at Nashville's Grand Ole Opry, and we were very proud to have had them as our club's Honorary Presidents. On a personal basis over the years I had the great pleasure of working with Miki and Griff on many occasions, and in many different venues. It really was a pleasure. They were a joy to work with, and when we got the chance I would sit for hours in the dressing room talking with them and hearing their stories about their times in the days of the Old Time Variety Theatres, and the music hall days. It was absolutely fascinating to listen to and it was an amazing insight into stage performers' lives back then. They met while singing in the George Mitchell Choir in 1947, and went on to become huge stars in popular and country music.

Away from the Lazyacre, I was still very busy playing the circuit. One of the entertainment agencies I did some work for contacted me;

Bernie Lewis of the Kama Agency told me that they had just started a brand new record label. Bernie asked me if I would be interested in recording an album on his new label; I told him that I would give it some thought. I knew that many of the artistes on the club scene carried their own LP's for sale at their gigs, and were very successful doing it. When I worked with artistes like Tony Goodacre and Keith Manifold I had always noticed how popular their merchandise was. I later phoned Bernie and told him I was up for it, and then I got down to selecting the songs I was going to record on the album. I decided to call the album *Tony Best – By Request*, and I intended to include some of the most requested songs from my stage act.

After much agonising I selected the fourteen songs I was going to record. My thinking went like this – *San Antonio Rose* was an old Bob Wills' song, and was the very first song I opened the show with on our first clubnight at Lazyacre. I included eight songs which were my most requested numbers at the time Don Williams' You're *My Best Friend*, The Bee Gees' *Words*, Patsy Cline's *Crazy*, Ronnie Milsap's *A Legend in my Time*, Larry Gatlin's *I Don't Want to Cry*, Slim Whitman's *China Doll*, Kris Kristofferson's *One Day at a Time* and the classic *Nobody's Child*. Most of these songs were all slowish ballads so to brighten the album up a bit I included two up-tempo Don Williams songs, *Some Broken Hearts Never Mend* and *Turn Out The Light, Love Me Tonight* and Kenny Rogers' very lively *Love, Or Something Like It*. I felt I had to put in a Merle Haggard song, so I went for the very popular *Today I Started Loving You Again*. Finally, there was by far my most requested number *The Old Rugged Cross*, a track which over the years sold more records for me than any other song. Bernie and I got together and booked musicians. Bernie's producer Alan Davies manned the recording desk, and we were ready to go. Shortly afterwards I picked up two thousand twelve inch LP's to put on sale at my live shows.

Just a week after I received my delivery of the albums I had a Saturday evening booking at the British Legion, Sutton Bridge near Spalding in Lincolnshire. Followed by the Sunday night in Newmarket at Pete Sayers' 'Grand Ole Opry' which was held in a converted cinema in the middle of town. I didn't know how many albums to take with me. I settled on taking two boxes of fifty. Might as well be optimistic! At my show at Sutton Bridge Jean sat with the records and sold twenty-eight LP's, which I was very happy with.

The following night at Newmarket I was closing the first half of the show, and running up to the interval. Before my last song I announced that I had my new album on sale, and went on to sing *The Old Rugged Cross* which got a great reception. Jean was with me once again, and she placed herself with my records in the aisle at the front of the stage. At the front of the other aisle was an assistant selling ice creams. There was a huge queue for the ice creams but Jean was standing all on her own. Then there was a rush. It seemed most of the ice cream queue had thought that their queue was for the records, and when they realised that it was not they came over to Jean. She sold seventy-one of the seventy-two records we had leaving just one in the box. As the interval came to an end Jean was returning to the back of the theatre when she was stopped by someone who said, 'Have you got any left?' Jean said, 'Just one,' and she sold the last one. What a result!

We knew that it wasn't always going to be like that but what a brilliant start as a recording artiste. We were excited to be back in Shrewsbury on the following evening for our fortnightly Monday show at Lazyacre – and hopefully more record sales!

CHAPTER 14

The Roadshow

After his appearance at Lazyacre I had kept in closer touch with Bob Newman. I had been talking to him after the Lazyacre show and he told me he had recommended me to an agent he knew. This agent booked the entertainment for a string of EMI Bingo Halls in the south of England. Bob regularly played some of these and he told me that they were good gigs to do. All the venues wanted from the artiste was a twenty minute spot during their interval and another twenty minute spot at the end of the evening. Whilst the artiste is singing two or three usherettes walk around the room with the artiste's records for sale. I thought what a great arrangement. As a result of Bob's kind recommendation I played quite a number of these bingo halls around Surrey, Sussex and Berkshire. Bob lived in Tilehurst just outside Reading, and while I was doing some of these gigs Bob invited me to stay at his house. We became good friends, and exchanged a lot of telephone numbers of venues which we thought would be of use to the other.

On one of these trips down south when I was staying with him Bob and I were chatting about the music scene. He suggested that maybe we could think about putting together a little roadshow featuring the two of us for a tour of country music clubs sometime. Bob had a great many contacts in Scotland, and he thought he could put together a couple of weeks work up there. He also knew a lot of places near his home in Reading and in the Oxford area. I had plenty of contacts in Norfolk and Lincolnshire and in North Wales and around the Midlands. The more we talked about it the more we thought it was a good idea. We decided we would try to put a couple of month's work together.

Bob was now working as a solo artiste and we kept on discussing the way we could put together our little roadshow. After hours of discussion we finally decided that for the sake of variety we could do with a girl on the show. We considered a number of girl singers who were on the country music scene, but none really appealed to us. That was until we thought of the young girl who had done a guest spot with us at Lazyacre, Carole Gordon. I said, 'I'll speak to her Mum and Dad,' which I did.

We thought back to that jam session at the end of the evening at Lazyacre when we noticed what a good harmony singer Carole was. We thought she could be the one we need to complete the line up. As well as having a superb voice she could strum a guitar and she was a very good keyboard player so she would be an asset to any show.

Carole had left school now. She was sixteen, and working in Millets the camping shop in Leek, and she was dying to get into the music business. Our idea of the way the show would run was for each of the three of us to do a solo spot, while for the second half of the show we would join forces and do the rest of the evening together. If we were in a dancing venue we could do the whole evening together. I often worked with a drummer so it would be a four-piece band.

I approached Carole's Mum and Dad. In fact Jean and I drove over to where they lived near Leek in North Staffordshire, and when we told them all what we had in mind Carole was dead keen. But Mum and Dad had some misgivings at first. However when they heard that Jean was travelling everywhere with us they were quite happy. They just didn't fancy their sixteen year old daughter travelling the country with three blokes! So as soon as they were put right on that issue Carole was pleased to join the team. We decided to call the show The Lazyacre Country Roadshow because that was where we all met for the first time.

We spent a few weeks rehearsing, whilst Bob and I were putting together the dates and venues for the first tour of the Roadshow. This first tour consisted of thirteen nights playing clubs in the north of Scotland from Tuesday through to a week the following Sunday. That way I was able to be at Lazyacre on the Monday before travelling through the night to appear in Aberdeen on the Tuesday. Then we did every single night until the second Sunday when we played Kinlochleven, near Fort William. After this show we travelled home through the night so that I could be at Lazyacre for the next show on the Monday.

This format worked really well, and we repeated it twice a year for three years in April and October. Each time we went to Scotland we hired a self-catering holiday cottage in a place called Alves near Elgin. Alves was mid way between Inverness and Aberdeen and very central for our work up there and it would be our base. As for the shows it was just like travelling from home to a one night stand. Our bookings up there were in Aberdeen, Inverness, Elgin, Invergordon, Inverurie, Peterhead, Bucksburn, Ardersier and even occasionally as far north as Thurso, which was only nineteen miles from John O'Groats!

The cottage was a holiday cottage owned by a company called Forres Estates, and as our tours were in April/May and October we didn't interfere with their summer season letting so we were able to rent it at a reasonable price. We used to travel in convoy in two Volvo Estates. Carole travelled with Jean and I in our car, whilst in the other car was Bob and George Foster our drummer.

When we got back from the Scotland tour we took a week off for a break, and then we did a week's tour of some of my old venues in North Wales including the Four Oaks Restaurant, Colwyn Bay and half a dozen venues on the Isle of Anglesey. Straight after this we travelled down south to do a week of shows near Bob's home in Reading, Wokingham, Slough and Kidlington near Oxford.

The Lazyacre Country Roadshow which was expected to be only a couple of month's work when Bob and I came up with the idea just grew and grew in popularity. Over the next twelve months we must have done at least a hundred shows all over this country and abroad – yes abroad! We were surprised and delighted to get a phone call from an agent in Northern Ireland Lou Rodgers (Clodagh Rodgers' Dad). One of his acts had worked with us at St. Peter's Catholic Club in Gloucester and had recommended us to him. He was putting together the entertainment programme for an International Music Festival at the Brann Football Stadium, Bergen in Norway.

He asked, 'Would we be interested in appearing on the festival?' 'Of course we would!' So the deal was done. We were to get a good fee, and return flights with two nights' accommodation in a good hotel. We were thrilled and especially delighted when we found out what the full line up of artistes was for the festival. Topping the bill were American country superstars Tompall and the Glaser Brothers.

Clodagh Rodgers and her band were going to be on, and there were two Norwegian country bands. Country Music was very big in Norway, and these two country bands were exceptionally good. They were Bjoro Haland and his band, and Teddy Nelson and his band. We were to be third on stage on the Sunday afternoon, after which we were able to enjoy the rest of the festival. We played for an hour to an enthusiastic audience of several thousand. We felt like we had hit the big time. It was a simply wonderful experience for Carole, Bob, George and I.

We toured extensively in the following couple of years with the Roadshow. We played all over the south of England, the West Country, East Anglia, Yorkshire and Lincolnshire, North Wales and of course our Scottish tours. We all became really close friends, and those days when the four of us and Jean toured together were some of the most enjoyable times we ever had on the road. I thought of including in this book some of the amusing and often hilarious moments during our times on tour with the Roadshow, but whatever I wrote it didn't seem as funny in print as it was at the time. You just had to be there. We certainly did have some great times and we were constantly laughing. The five of us Carole, Bob, George, Jean and I were a great team. Not only did we work well together on stage but on a personal basis we were great friends, and loved our times together.

For many years afterwards, every time I was on the same show with Carole and Bob we always got together for what we called a Roadshow spot. Despite not having rehearsed together we could drop into the old routine straight away. Every time Carole and Bob appeared at Lazyacre over the years we did the same. It just brought back to us those good times on the road together – and the audiences loved it as well!

When we first started the Roadshow I insisted on one rule, and that was that there was to be no romance within the group. I had seen it so often with bands; when two members of a band get together and form an alliance. When they eventually fall out and split up, nine times out of ten, the whole band collapses because they can no longer work together. So I insisted. No romance within the group - and everyone accepted that. So I was happy.

On the final night of our Scottish tours Carole would travel home with Jean and me because we could drop her off at Knutsford Services on the M6 where her Mum and Dad would pick her up. George who lived at Cannock would travel with Bob because Bob's journey took him very close to George's house on his way home to Reading. It worked well every time.

It was the final night of one of these Scottish tours when we were playing at Clachnacuddin Football Club in Inverness. When it came to the end of the night, and we were loading the cars to come home Carole put her guitar into Bob's car. When I saw this I said, 'Carole, you've made a mistake. That guitar needs to go into my car.' Carole blushed, and said, 'No, I'm going home with Bob tonight.' I saw what was happening and I went through the roof! 'This will be the end of the Roadshow. I warned you about this.' By now everything was loaded into the cars. I couldn't do anything about it. Carole went with Bob. George travelled with Jean and me. I was seething. I could see our precious Roadshow collapsing in front of my very eyes.

In the end it all turned out alright. I might have overreacted because Carole and Bob were both single. They went out together for a few years before they eventually got married, and they spent a very happy twenty-five years together before Bob's untimely passing in April 2014 from cancer of the Oesophagus. Carole's initial reaction to the devastating loss of Bob was to quit the music business, but one of Bob's final requests to Carole was that she should not give up, but to continue singing. I am delighted to say she still tours with her stunning tribute to The Carpenters 'Voice of the Heart,' and their lively pop and country touring show, 'Forever in Blue Jeans.' We are all very sad at the loss of Bob, and we wish Carole continued success in her already successful musical career. I am so pleased she is continuing with her career in music. She is far too talented not to make use of her wonderful gift.

CHAPTER 15

On the Road

The next few years were among the busiest times of my life as far as being a travelling entertainer was concerned. Since the move from Anglesey to Shropshire in 1975 it had taken me a couple of years to get myself established in my new local area of Shropshire. I took anything and everything that was offered to me in the way of work simply to fill the diary. I felt that once the diary was pretty full that was the time to start being selective about what work to accept, and not before. The policy worked and by 1979 I was very happy to be an extremely busy artiste.

I was very keen to travel the country, and I was lucky enough to work with some more established artistes on the road. In these early days as a pro artiste I did quite a few shows with a singer who became a great friend, Keith Manifold. Keith had done it all. He had appeared on television on Hughie Green's *Opportunity Knocks* (finishing second to series winner Lena Zavaroni.) He had albums on sale, and had picked up a recording contract with DJM the Nashville recording label. He really was established. We worked together a lot, and Keith gave me a number of pointers as to who to approach for the right kind of work in the business.

In fact Keith and I were working together in the Monkmoor Hotel in Shrewsbury on August 16th 1977 the night Elvis Presley died. We had a very lively crowd in that night, and we had each done one spot and were taking a break before the second half of the show. During that break the news came through that Elvis had passed away in his home in Memphis, Tennessee. After our break I opened with a couple of songs, and then I introduced Keith. We both found it really hard going. We simply could not lift the crowd. The sad news seemed to have stunned everyone, and the evening had lost all the great atmosphere that was there in the first half. When it came to my spot because I knew about a dozen Elvis songs I decided to sing them all as a sort of tribute. I had always sung a few Elvis numbers in my show. In fact as a joke I used to announce, 'I'm going to sing an Elvis Presley song, and all the time I'm singing this song, I'll be doing the actions just like Elvis. You can't see them but underneath these trousers, they'll be going on all the time I'm singing!'

In later years Keith became my stage manager for Tony Best Leisure for a long time until we sadly lost him to a sudden heart attack at one of our TBL events in Sussex in May 2005. He was just fifty-eight. I still cannot drive past the Monkmoor Hotel in Shrewsbury without thinking of Keith. He had been a wonderful friend, and I still miss him today.

I was also fortunate enough to be booked for a three week tour with rock and roll legend Wee Willie Harris and his band. Willie was a real character and a great entertainer. He used to do all the old rock and roll standards, but also threw in a few jokes for good measure and was a really good entertainer. I also did a memorable two weeks with a fabulous singer who was another terrific entertainer Frank Ifield. Frank was a real gentleman and a delight to work with. His backing musicians were a country band from Northamptonshire, Barbary Coast.

When it got to the stage where I could afford to be a bit more selective about my work I had several irons in the fire. I had done my residencies at the medieval banquets and the pub at Eccleshall. I now had the Lazyacre and the Lazyacre Roadshow. My work as a solo entertainer was taking me all over the country. There was a tremendous amount of driving which Jean and I shared. We went through three Volvo Estates in the eighties, two of which did well over 100,000 miles before we changed them. The third one would have done that much as well if we had not had it written off in a collision on the M5 when we were travelling to a show down in Gloucester.

There was a tailback on our carriageway because of a crash caused by drivers looking at another accident on the other side of the motorway, I think they call it rubbernecking. Anyway we were stationary behind a big Wincanton Haulage wagon when Jean said, 'Brace yourself. He's not going to stop.' She was looking behind at a white van that was approaching us at high speed. He must have still been doing fifty when he hit us, pushing us into the back of the Wincanton wagon.

When everything had settled down and the van driver had gone off in an ambulance we were towed off the motorway. Our car doors wouldn't open as we were squeezed up front and back. Jean and I got out of the car through the windows, and the AA relayed us back to Shrewsbury dropping the car off at the Volvo Centre before taking us home. We considered ourselves very lucky. We were driving about forty thousand miles a year and doing as many as three hundred one night stands a year, so the law of averages says you are going to have a bump sometime. It was very scary though, but we weren't hurt. The car was a complete write-off though.

Although my diary was full Jean and I were able to get away for a two week working holiday abroad after an agent, Lee Williams, phoned me and offered me a fortnights working holiday in the Dolmen Hotel, St. Paul's Bay, Malta. The arrangement was that we got our flights, accommodation and all our meals free and I would get £100 each week spending money. For this I had to do two spots of forty-five minutes each on five evenings a week. It was a great offer and one we took up without any hesitation. The hotel had the sound equipment and microphones. All I needed to take was my accordion. The sound equipment was very antiquated but it served its purpose as I was not playing to a big room. It was more like a pub lounge. As well as me they had a little local trio playing for dancing from eight until midnight every night.

When we left England Lynne was expecting Beverley, her second daughter, but the baby was not due for two or three more weeks. Sod's law! Beverley was born the day after we flew to Malta, and we had to wait what seemed a long two weeks to see our new granddaughter. As I was only singing in the evenings for that fortnight in the Dolmen Hotel we hired a car and explored every inch of this beautiful island. We got to really love Malta, and we went back there several times on holiday in later years.

Back home we seemed to be permanently on the road. My work had gone from the pubs and social clubs to many more country music clubs and theatre shows. But a booking in Herne Bay, Kent at the end of 1978 led to a great opportunity for me, and one lunchtime booking at Pontin's, Hemsby in Norfolk turned out to be very significant, and changed my direction once again.

This is a case in point as to how useful it can be to be available to do some work for entertainment agencies. The booking in Kent was the result of a phone call from Scotland's Drew Taylor Agency and the booking at Pontin's was arranged for me by the Mike and Margaret Storey Agency in Yorkshire. Both these bookings opened important doors for me and were pivotal in my career in the following few years.

CHAPTER 16

Summer Seasons

Toward the back end of 1978 I was booked to do two shows at the King's Hall, Herne Bay in Kent. One was as part of the Bill Grant and Delia Bell bluegrass tour organised by a promoter from Walsall, Don Page, and the other was a one-off booking I received through an agent in Scotland, Drew Taylor, who had been booking the King's Hall summer season artistes that year.

At the end of my second booking there I was approached by the management of the King's Hall, and they asked me if I would be interested in playing there for a mini summer season the following year. I was asked if I could do every Tuesday, Wednesday and Thursday from the beginning of June through to the middle of September 1979. The fees on offer were very good and the arrangement suited me perfectly. I would have to find some accommodation for the three days I was there, but there were plenty of good B&B's available. The booking wouldn't interfere with my Monday nights at Lazyacre, and it left me every Friday, Saturday and Sunday free to obtain work elsewhere on the three busiest nights of the week. So I was pleased to accept their offer for my very first summer season.

The three nights all had different themes. On the Tuesday evenings we had a family entertainment show with me as the host. We booked various special guest artistes and the whole evening's programme was sponsored by P & O Ferries, whose offices were in Dover, who supplied us with loads of prizes for the children and some for the Mums and Dads. It was a non-stop all action evening a bit like a holiday camp show, and it turned out to be very popular with local families as well as with visiting families on holiday.

Wednesday was a country music show on which I opened the show with a solo spot followed by a resident country band. This resident band spot was shared by two Kent based bands with alternate Wednesdays being done by The Garry Blackmore Band and the Ned Porridge Band, featuring Eddie Pearson.

After the band's spot I would introduce a special guest star who would top the bill. These bill toppers included The Duffy Brothers, Jeannie Denver & the JD Band, top American fiddle player Billy Armstrong, Tammy Cline, Joe Brown, Wally Whyton, Lonnie Donegan and Miki and Griff. These Wednesday country shows were very well supported, not least because the Gary Blackmore and Ned Porridge bands both had a great local following.

Finally on the Thursday evening I hosted a dance night. Once again I opened the evening with a short spot. Then we had a resident dance band and a guest singer. P & O Ferries supplied me with plenty of spot prizes so the three evenings provided a variety of entertainment, and the three shows were totally different to each other. It was an excellent three month contract for me as well as being tremendously enjoyable. For the three days each week I stayed in a comfortable Bed and Breakfast place where the couple from Liverpool who ran it treated me like one of the family, and I could come and go as I pleased.

The Kings Hall is a beautiful concert venue right on the sea front of the lovely old fashioned Victorian style resort of Herne Bay, and it was always a pleasure to play there. Herne Bay is situated about five miles along the coast from the busy harbour and fishing port of Whitstable which is well known as the 'Oyster Capital of England.' I have always loved being on the coast. I was born and brought up by the sea and it has always had a strong attraction for me. It is the only thing I miss living in Shrewsbury, but at least we live close enough to pay regular visits to the coast in North Wales.

We had a great summer season, and the fact that two of the three shows were sponsored by P & O Ferries gave me an additional fringe benefit. P & O owned a double-decker courtesy bus which during Kent County Cricket Club's home matches would be parked just outside the boundary of the St Lawrence Ground, Canterbury Kent's county ground. It was somewhere that celebrities and guests could view the match from the upstairs lounge with plenty of tea, coffee and light refreshments available downstairs. Playing at the Kings Hall in the evenings, of course, I was free every day during the daytime and after being given a complimentary free pass by P&O I spent many an enjoyable afternoon watching the cricket and talking to the other guests.

I particularly remember spending a pleasant afternoon chatting to former Yorkshire and Leicestershire bowler and former captain of England, Ray Illingworth upstairs on the bus. This was a real thrill for me.

The unique, and it really was unique, feature of the St Lawrence Ground was the fact that it had a large ninety foot lime tree located actually inside the boundary of play. The ground is one of the oldest in the country and was opened in 1847 and built around the tree. Special rules had to be introduced: if a batsman's shot touched any part of the tree it counted as four runs. Only four cricketers ever cleared the tree to score a six! Sad to say, in the 1990s the tree developed heart rot, and in 2005 high winds snapped the two hundred year old tree in two. So Canterbury's unique feature is no more, and it is no longer an interesting talking point to anyone visiting the ground for the first time.

Being free during the daytime also gave me the chance to check out the local area, and I spent a lot of time visiting the local villages and towns along the north Kent coast including Whitstable, Margate and Cliftonville. I visited the Medway towns of Chatham, Rochester and Gillingham, my Dad's home town. I spent hours one day in Gillingham looking for the street where my Dad lived, Jeyes Road, but I could not find it.

All these things helped to make it a memorable and most enjoyable summer season for me and I was thrilled when, at the end of the season, the management of the King's Hall invited me to do something similar there the following summer. The following year was going to be just two nights a week because P & O Ferries were not involved any more, but two nights suited me fine and it was still more than worthwhile doing. The country music night was to continue as in the previous year featuring myself opening the show and the two resident bands on alternate weeks, and a special star guest to top the bill. On the following night I once again hosted a star cabaret evening, and we had yet another successful season at this beautiful venue.

These two years were the only time I ever did summer seasons. I had offers for others, but I found them too difficult to fit in with my work at the festivals and my fortnightly Lazyacre club. On occasions I was able to do a midweek night every week through the summer at a venue. That sort of thing did not interfere with my other work.

One such booking was for every Wednesday through the summer season one year at Venue Cymru the North Wales Theatre in Llandudno. It was a weekly variety evening featuring a line up of all Welsh artistes. I compered the show and provided the comedy element. Resident with me were Iona and Andy who had a terrific following on the North Wales coast, and there were guest artistes of choirs, harpists and singers, all well known to a Welsh audience. The shows were well advertised in the North Wales newspapers and in the *Holyhead and Anglesey Mail,* and they drew great crowds. As it had been some years since I left the area it was a great pleasure to see a number of acquaintances and old friends who knew me from my time living in Anglesey. That brought back a lot of memories.

CHAPTER 17

The Pontin's Years

Early in 1979 I was booked to appear at a Sunday lunchtime show at Pontin's Holiday Village, Hemsby on the Norfolk coast. It turned out to be a very important booking for me. The event was a brand new venture which Pontin's were just starting – residential country music festivals. The festival director was Mr Bob Chapple and they called the events Pontin's 'Country Style' Festivals, and this event was the first of them. Responsible for booking artistes and bands was Pontin's booking agent, Miss Bridie Reid, and she had booked me through a specialist country music agency based in Yorkshire, the Mike and Margaret Storey Agency.

With an audience of about a thousand my spot on stage went very well, and when I had finished I was in the dressing room when one of the Pontin's Bluecoats called in, and asked me to come over to the bar to meet Miss Bridie Reid. I followed him to the bar, and he introduced me to Miss Reid. She complimented me on my show and asked me if I would be interested in doing some more work for the company. Of course I said I would love to, and she told me that they would be presenting five of their Country Style festivals each year. There were to be two full self-catering weeks here at Hemsby, two similar full weeks at Brean Sands, near Burnham-on-Sea in Somerset. Finally there was to be one week each April at their Tower Beach Holiday Village in Prestatyn on the North Wales coast.

After we had chatted for a while she offered me the job of compere and entertainer at all of these festivals for the following year. I needed to do a bit of rearranging of some dates in my diary, but this was far too good an offer to refuse. Pontin's would pay me a good fee for each of the events, provide me with accommodation and free electricity, and my food was available in the staff canteen. There was a show every lunchtime, and of course each evening. I was to arrange the running order and to compere these shows. There would also be a couple of spots for me to do during the week, and any time there was a delay I could be on hand to fill in where necessary. This sounded absolutely perfect for me and I jumped at the chance to be associated with a huge firm like Pontin's. It turned out to be a really good move for me.

The Pontin's Empire also owned a company offering holidays abroad – 'Go-Pontinental,' later called Holiday Club International. They had resorts all over Europe and in Tenerife. Bridie Reid said to me that anytime I fancied two weeks in the sun just let her know. She could offer me an arrangement she had with a number of artistes. There was no money in it, but flights and full board accommodation would be free for Jean and me and the family, and I would be required to do a forty-five minute cabaret spot on two evenings each week. They would also pay me £50 each week toward my expenses. It sounded like a good deal to me, and I took her up on the offer several times in the following few years.

I started off by doing two weeks over the New Year period at their Ten Bel resort in Tenerife, and in all I did three consecutive New Year breaks. Over the next three years I did two week breaks in Cala Mesquida, Majorca, Torremolinos and Estepona on mainland Spain, and in their resort on the island of Sardinia in the Mediterranean. Though it was not a money spinner it saved me forking out for holidays for the family, and we all loved it. We did not enjoy Sardinia very much but the ones I did at their centres in Spain and Tenerife were just brilliant. It was not something I could do very often because I had a living to make, but a couple of times a year was ideal for us.

When I did these working holidays there were usually three or four other acts doing the same thing in the same weeks as me. Obviously with me being their cabaret act on one night each week they needed other artistes to fill a few other nights in the week. It was at the first New Year break I did at Ten Bel that among the artistes appearing was a fantastic comedy double act. They were called Don D. Williams and Doreen Savage. Doreen was a lovely singer of country songs and songs from the shows *Don't Cry for me, Argentina*, etc. Don was just an immensely funny man. He was a great comedy act without telling jokes. It was all really to do with audience participation. We saw them again the following year for the New Year break at Ten Bel.

Jean and I got on really well with Don and Doreen, and some years later when they were spending some time in the UK, between Tenerife contracts, I got them a bit of work over here. They even did a couple of shows at Lazyacre. Don was just a nutter, but what an entertainer; they were just hilarious. Poor Doreen had to put up with a lot, but our club members loved them. They even won our 'Most Popular Show' award in 1988.

As far as the Pontin's 'Country Style' festivals in the UK were concerned they were hard work, but very enjoyable events to do. They were very well supported with two or three thousand guests at each one. There were two entertainment halls at each centre. One was the concert hall, and the other the dance hall aimed at those who wanted to dance all night. Resident with me at all the festivals was another compere to share those duties with me. Usually it was Gerry Ford from Edinburgh, but sometimes it was Vic Woodhouse of the band Hickory Lake who would sometimes be one of the resident bands. Other bands who did residencies were Burnt Ash, West Virginia and the Yorkshire based band Mustang. The resident country music DJ for all the festivals was the very flamboyant Ian Ashcroft from Southport who was immensely popular, and to complete the line up there was Tone Howard who was our resident square-dance caller.

All the best known artistes and bands on the British country music scene appeared regularly on these festivals as well as many star names and visiting artistes from the USA and Europe. These were really big, high profile events; for an artiste just to appear on one of the Pontin's festivals was a feather in the cap. So for me to be resident on all of them – I felt like I had hit the jackpot! I enjoyed the work, and my record sales were phenomenal.

In addition to the entertainment rooms there was an area in the main complex where they accommodated about half a dozen trade stands where records and cassettes were on sale, there were no CD's then!, several western gear stands and leathercraft stands. It all enhanced the atmosphere of the whole thing. When I was not on stage I used to join Bill and Martin the two chaps who ran the record stall. They were directors of a London firm I & B Records selling British, American and Irish records and tapes, and they had a very attractive stand at all the Pontin's festivals. Artistes who were appearing through the week could put their albums on sale on the stand, and of course I had my own albums on sale there. By spending most of my spare time with Bill and Martin on the stand all the guests became aware of where to find me if they had a problem. Artistes who had just appeared on stage would join us on the record stand to sign albums for fans and they did great business just by giving that extra bit of time.

I continued to do these festivals for just over four years until I decided I wanted a change. I felt that the music side of these festivals was becoming less important, and the emphasis was becoming more and more on the 'Cowboy' element with their 'Fast Draw Competitions,' mock battles, shoot-outs and the various re-enactments of the American Civil War and such like. All these things were very spectacular, but not of any interest to me. I was a music person! So I decided to move on and I went back to being on the road full time as a travelling entertainer.

CHAPTER 18

Tragedy

Of course in addition to the summer season work and the Pontin's festivals I still had my regular work which took me all over England and Wales, and of course the twice a year visits to Scotland. I had a strong base back in Shropshire with the fortnightly shows at Lazyacre, and a lot of small venues which I had loyalty to after being looked after by them in the early days. The New Inn at Prees and The More Arms at Minsterley spring to mind.

In 1981 we moved house from Bayston Hill to Lancaster Road on the north side of town. The house and the location were more suitable to our needs. It was also closer to Lynne and her family who lived on that side of town. I converted the small bedroom into an office where I kept all my paperwork, diaries and accounts. It gave me a good base to work from. By this time I had a second album on sale along with *Tony Best – By Request* which was still selling well. The second album was called *Sincerely – Tony Best*, and I recorded it at a studio near Oxford with some great musicians and backing vocals by Bob and Carole.

In May 1982 I returned from a festival week at Brean Sands followed by two one night stands on the Saturday and Sunday in Yorkshire, getting home to Shrewsbury about 3 am on the Monday morning. I got up about nine and had breakfast with Jean then went into the office to get my week's paperwork sorted out.

About eleven that morning we received the upsetting news that our son, Mark, had suffered an accident at work. Mark worked for a local industrial cleaning company, and he had been cleaning second floor windows at Harper Adams College, Newport, near Telford. He had fallen off his ladder and had been taken to the Royal Shrewsbury Hospital. We contacted the hospital to be told the devastating news that he had been pronounced dead on arrival. Mark was just 21 years old and due to be married to his fiancée Hazel two weeks later.

Our lives had just fallen apart. Jean was totally inconsolable as was Lynne who was devoted to her brother, and the bottom had just fallen out of our world. I am not going to go into this in any more detail; it hurts too much. Suffice it to say it was simply the worst time of our lives.

My act on stage consisted of singing songs and telling a few jokes, and my thoughts were, 'I'm never going to be able to do that again,' such were my feelings of despair. I knew that I would have to eventually, but I also knew I would have to give myself a lot of time before getting back to work. The venue organisers I was booked for were all more than sympathetic and just told me to give it as much time as I needed.

For my return to the stage some time later I chose a booking where I knew I would have great support. I was booked to appear at the Theatre Royal, Bury St Edmunds in Suffolk to appear with Bob, Carole and George as the Lazyacre Roadshow, with special guest star guests Miki and Griff. It could not have been a better show to get back into business.

Jean came with me, and after the loss of Mark she had no desire to be at home on her own so she travelled with me everywhere I went after that. We were a good team and a great comfort to each other on those inevitable moments when we were down. Being on the road most of the time we always looked forward to getting back home for a few days to catch up on Lynne and her two little ones Michelle and Beverley.

I make no bones about it - the show at Bury St Edmunds was very hard, but I had great support from the others and hopefully we gave the audience a super show. The first time back was definitely the hardest, but it did get better after that, and with Jean by my side it was so much easier.

As I write this it is over thirty-three years since we lost our son. We have his picture at the top of our stairs and we say hello to him every day. What we have lost in our son we have more than made up for in our amazing daughter, Lynne, who is now our carer!!! – and of course our wonderful grandchildren and great grandchildren.

CHAPTER 19

Lazyacre Holidays

Lazyacre Country Music Club was, and still is, always more than just a concert once every two weeks. Although the fortnightly concerts are very important, and from the beginning we have always tried to present a top notch entertainment programme, the club has developed into a meeting place and social gathering. Our members, as well as enjoying the shows on our clubnights, also enjoy sharing interests and taking part in special events and trips. Everyone knows each other and it is more like a family getting together for a fortnightly catch up. We open the doors at 5pm and there are members waiting for us then. By 5:30pm we are usually half full, yet the show doesn't start until 8pm! It's amazing. They all enjoy that get together at the start of the evening. Some have food, others just a drink, but the place is alive with people just meeting up with their friends; it is brilliant.

When the club had been running about two years some of our members suggested we organise a club holiday abroad. So it was May 1980 when sixty-three members of the club came to Spain for a wonderful ten day holiday in Benidorm. We stayed at the Hotel Fenicia in the centre of Benidorm's old town, and we had a really fabulous time. Flights, full board, insurance and coaches to and from the airport both ends – all for £183.00! This was the first of many Lazyacre holidays abroad and around Britain, and it was the forerunner of many such holidays for a group of friends who just loved each other's company.

In 1981 we had no less than three Lazyacre holidays. In May we went to the Hotel Magalluf Park in Majorca, in September it was the four-star Hotel Fortina in Sliema, Malta, and in October 150 Lazyacre members and friends attended one of the Pontin's 'Country Style' Festivals at Brean Sands in Somerset. These were three excellent holidays. The following year fifty of us went back to Benidorm this time to the Hotel Presidente in the new part of the town. We also took large numbers to Pontin's festivals in Prestatyn and Brean Sands.

In 1983 and 1984 we took about sixty members on each occasion to country music sunshine holidays presented by Go-Pontinental at their resorts in Cala Mesquida, Majorca in 1983, and in Torremolinos in 1984. Our Lazyacre party on these two holidays included about a dozen of our handicapped Lazyacre members who were resident in Kyre Park House, Tenbury Wells, Worcestershire. This was a superb stately home owned by the Spastics Society. The Kyre Park residents loved their country music, and they were always happy to travel the forty miles to come to Shrewsbury for our clubnights. The residents, and their carers, were regular and enthusiastic visitors to the club.

In the summer of 1988 we took our first Lazyacre coach holiday when fifty of us went to the north of Scotland. Due to the popularity of this type of holiday we presented a week long summer coach holiday every year for the following twenty years to a number of different destinations.

Over the years we visited the north of Scotland three more times, and we had great holidays in County Kerry in Ireland, Bournemouth, Stirling and central Scotland, Scarborough (no less than five times – a favourite resort with our party), Suffolk and the Norfolk Broads, Sussex by the Sea, The Isle of Wight, Blackpool and the Lake District and twice to Weston-super-Mare.

I am sure that spending these holidays together brought our club members much closer to each other, which could only enhance the atmosphere within the club. Each one of these holidays had its own individual memorable moments; we would often recall these to each other from time to time. Do you remember when this happened, or so and so did this? These holidays gave everyone who came on them common experiences to share.

For the first couple of Scottish holidays we took we stayed in Inverness, and because the hotels in the city were out of our price range we stayed at a number of Bed and Breakfast places which had been recommended by friends at the Inverness Country & Western Club. We had between six and twelve of our party in each of these establishments (private homes), so we were staying in five or six different houses all quite close to each other. For our day trips out the coach would pick up at each of the B&B's before we actually got under way on the trip that day.

Our excursions were to musical evenings at theatres or country music clubs. We visited Elgin Country Music Club, but we went in the morning so that during the day we could take in Pringle's Edinburgh Woollen Mill in Elgin and Baxters Foods in Fochabers, near Elgin. We learned just how they processed their soups, jams and marmalades and numerous other items all of which were on sale in the factory shop after our tour. We then went to a hotel where we had 'high tea', a Scottish speciality, before going on to the St Leonards Hotel for an evening at the country music club. We also took in a trip to a whisky distillery and to an authentic Scottish show in the Cummings Hotel, Inverness and a Ceilidh in the Eden Court Theatre, Inverness. On the three occasions we took a holiday in Inverness we never missed the opportunity to take an evening cruise on the Jacobite Cruiser on Loch Ness with entertainment by either John C. King or Jolene and Barry, and a delicious hot supper of another Scottish delicacy, stovies on our way back from the two hour cruise. This was always one of the highlights of the holiday. We never saw Nessie!

Another of the holidays we took in Scotland was in Fort William when we stayed at the Croit Anna Hotel on the shores of Loch Linnhe just five miles from Ben Nevis. Fort William is sixty-five miles south of Inverness so we were able to include some different excursions including a memorable one to Seil Island just twelve miles south of Oban off the western edge of the Scottish mainland.

To get to the island the coach had to take us over the very small Clachan Bridge better known as the 'Bridge over the Atlantic' because it crosses the inlet of the Atlantic Ocean which makes Seil Island an actual island. Before crossing the bridge our driver announced that unfortunately the bridge wasn't considered strong enough to take a fully loaded coach so we would all have to get off the coach to walk across the bridge, and allow the coach to go over empty; then we could get back on board! Everyone did as they were told, and once on the other side we all got back on the coach. On arrival at the tourist attraction on the island we were all piped off the coach by a lone piper in his Highland Dress.

We had some refreshments and visited the huge gift and souvenir shop before boarding the coach for the return journey. As we approached the bridge over the Atlantic it was clear our driver had no intention of stopping. There were screams from the back of the coach, 'Aren't you going to stop?' The driver answered into his microphone, 'No. I'm just going to take a chance!' And he carried on, crossed the bridge safely and took us back to Fort William with half his passengers still thinking we were lucky not to be in the Atlantic!

One of the favourite resorts for our Lazyacre holidaymakers was Scarborough on the North Yorkshire coast. We always stayed at the Delmont Hotel a very homely private hotel situated on the cliffs with a stunning view over the North Bay. It had everything we needed. Comfortable rooms, excellent food and wonderful service.

We were very much at home there.

Each time we went to Scarborough we always did more or less the same things, but everybody loved it. During the week we always took in theatre shows at the Spa Theatre and at the YMCA Theatre for what was always a brilliant show put on by local youngsters. Sometimes we would visit the Spa Theatre at Bridlington, seventeen miles away.

Our excursions were also very predictable, but nonetheless always enjoyable. Sunday mornings we would visit the quaint little fishing port of Whitby and the Whitby fish and chips for lunch were a must. We always took a trip through the beautiful Yorkshire Dales and often the North Yorkshire Moors and Heartbeat Country. On our final evening at the Delmont we would always book an artiste to entertain us at our farewell party in the restaurant which was converted into a concert room for the evening with a stage and lighting. The following morning all the hotel staff would be on the steps of the hotel to wave us off on our journey home. It was simply great. Just sitting here writing about it makes me want to go back there now!

We always seemed to get good weather – of course it was always the second week in August so we could expect it to be good. We only came unstuck with the weather once.

That was on our holiday to the Isle of Wight in 2008. It just poured with rain for the whole week. We were lucky that we were staying at one of Warner's centres - Norton Grange Holiday Village at Yarmouth on the island so there was plenty of entertainment for us to enjoy on site with a good entertainments team and visiting cabaret artistes. So we didn't let the rain spoil our holiday. We did try to get out and about, but when we visited The Needles, we nearly got blown off the cliff overlooking them, and when we visited Newport we only got off the coach for half an hour to get a drink and a snack in a pub, then back on the coach to shelter from the driving rain. But that was only once in about twenty years.

The regular members of our group who used to come on these holidays particularly enjoyed our visits north of the border. We had previously always gone right up north to Inverness or Fort William so one year we decided to have a change and pay a visit to central Scotland. We stayed in the city of Stirling at the very comfortable Golden Lion Hotel where we were well looked after. As this was an area we had not been to before we were able to arrange excursions to plenty of new places. We visited the impressive Stirling Castle, the Wallace Monument, Loch Lomond and the Trossachs. We spent a really lovely day in Edinburgh. In the morning we had a conducted tour around the Royal Yacht Britannia, and we spent all afternoon in this stunning city. Many of us took a trip on the tourist hop on/hop off double-decker bus for a tour of the city with a most interesting commentary.

Because we always packed so much into these holidays it was our policy to have a free day on the Tuesday or Wednesday to give everyone time to recharge batteries, or to have a leisurely look around wherever we were staying. However this time our coach driver suggested that as we were so close it would be remiss of us not to visit the Falkirk Wheel. I, for one, had never even heard of the Falkirk Wheel, but the driver insisted that it was something not to be missed. He was quite right.

The whole structure is simply amazing. It is a rotating boat lift connecting the Forth and Clyde Canal with the Union Canal. It was only opened in 2002. The wheel raises or lowers boats by a massive thirty-six feet which is the difference in levels between the two canals. Prior to the opening of the wheel narrowboats, barges and pleasure craft travelling between Edinburgh and Glasgow had to manoeuvre their way through a staircase of eleven locks. This transit took almost a whole day to complete. The Falkirk Wheel does the same job in about half an hour! I can thoroughly recommend a visit to see this phenomenon to anyone who finds themselves within reach of it. It is a simply awesome tourist attraction.

Another club holiday took us to stay at Warner's Gunton Hall, near Lowestoft, and the holiday included a pleasure cruise on the Norfolk Broads with live entertainment by Dave Bryan on the boat. We also went a couple of times to Blackpool and the Lakes taking in some of the fantastic summer shows in this lively resort, and a cruise on Lake Windermere with a delicious cream tea at Ambleside. Other excursions included a day in Southport and a trip to Lancaster Castle with a wonderful guided tour and a most enthusiastic commentary.

My affinity with Weston-super-Mare since my early days in the RAF prompted me to arrange a couple of our Lazyacre summer holidays there - one in 2009 and our final one in 2013. Knowing the resort so well I knew that our members would just love it. We chose a very nice small hotel on the sea front, the New Ocean Hotel, which Jean and I checked out by booking a weekend there before booking the club holiday. The rooms were comfortable the food was excellent and the staff were very welcoming. That was all we needed.

During the week we took in shows in the Playhouse Theatre, one starring Val Doonican who was just brilliant, and the other was the lively touring show *That'll be the Day*. We also went to a couple of shows at the Winter Gardens which brought back happy memories for me of the days when I used to dance there in the 1950s as a young airman.

There were also plenty of places to visit on our coach excursions such as Lynton and Lynmouth, the city of Bath, Wells Cathedral, Clevedon, and a wonderful farm near Bristol called Oakham Treasures which had three big outbuildings packed to the rafters with antiques and collectibles. It had everyone remembering their childhood.

Our 2013 holiday there was going to be the last one which Jean and I organised, and I booked an excellent artiste, Morgan Reeves from North Wales, to play for our final party night on the Friday. Morgan was superb as usual. I was going to sing a few songs during Morgan's break, but I was told to sit still and allow our daughter Lynne to bring Morgan off as she wanted to make an announcement. It was not just any announcement. Unbeknown to us the members on our trip had got together and held a collection for Jean and me to thank us for all the wonderful holidays we had arranged. We were speechless; it was a lovely gesture. Jean thanked them all. I couldn't speak! Their generosity paid for a three day break in London for us; we stayed near Covent Garden and went to see two theatre shows in the West End. We even had afternoon tea at the Ritz! It was a memorable few days for us. Lynne came with us too because we had to have our carer so we treated her to that.

The Lazyacre annual summer holiday meant a lot to us, and it is an important contributor to the feel good factor which we have at our club. All those who were with us on these holidays over the past twenty years certainly have a lot of wonderful memories to savour. The holidays were all very special to Jean and me and we loved every one of them.

CHAPTER 20

Touring

Jean and I loved touring the country though when I look back at my old diaries from the early eighties I wonder just how we did it. We certainly could not have done it with the amount of traffic and roadworks you see today. I noticed in my diary one weekend when I was in Sutton Bridge, near Spalding on the Saturday then 250 miles to Cleator Moor near the west coast of Cumbria on the Sunday, and then 210 miles home afterwards. The following week I played Lode, near Cambridge on the Sunday, Holyhead (250 miles away) on the Monday, and then we drove 320 miles to Ringwood in Hampshire to play there on the Tuesday. That is what you call being on the road! Of course it was not always like that. Five times a year we had a week at Pontin's with no travelling so that gave us the chance to recharge our batteries. We also had some specials, like three days in the Hilton Hotel, Rotterdam with Poacher, Tammy Cline and the Bob McKinlay Band. Travel was by coach and ferry via Felixstowe.

There were occasions when I could string four or five bookings together in the same area. One of these areas was in the West Country when I could put together Tuesday right through to the weekend without a lot of travelling. I would play the Sandy Cove Hotel near Ilfracombe on the Tuesday, The Lord Haldon Hotel, Dunchideock, near Exeter on the Wednesday, Culbone Stables, Porlock on the Thursday and Wellworthy Social Club, Bridgwater on the Friday.

I still had my contacts in North Wales and Anglesey and I could often do a few bookings in the same area up there. It also gave me the chance to catch up with old friends and my former band colleagues from the Midnight Sun days. In fact there were about five gigs in the Holyhead area which I could often rely upon. Another good area for me to link a few dates together was south Yorkshire, Derbyshire and Nottinghamshire. It was mainly working men's clubs and the occasional country music venue, but it was still enjoyable. They are great people up in that area. It is quite strange how you can catch on in one area while fifty miles up the road, they have never heard of you. I suppose you just need to put yourself about to get known. Of course when you are travelling the country playing and singing in so many different venues you are bound to have favourite places to do your thing. The types of places where we entertainers ply our trade are many and varied. Some venues suit a particular act and some do not.

For instance if I was playing in what we called a dancing venue, where the audience loved to dance from the word go, then I would tailor my act for that evening to include a minimum of chat and as much music as I could pack in. Although I could cope with this type of situation I did not feel the paying customers were getting the best of me, and there were many more artistes on the scene who could have done a better job than me for this kind of crowd. But I must have been doing something right for them otherwise I would not have received the percentage of return bookings that I did.

I was much more suited to the clubs we called concert clubs where for the most part the audience sat and listened, and were prepared to be entertained by the artiste. Fortunately for me during the time that I was on the road the vast majority of clubs, especially the country music clubs, were just my sort of venues. Very often toward the end of an evening guests would get up and have a dance, but for most of the show they just wanted to sit and be entertained.

I loved to interact with an audience finding out what sort of music they liked, who their favourite artistes were, so that I could tailor my act to keep them all happy. After all it is their evening out. I always included an element of comedy into the act particularly early on in a show. I was quite happy to sing and play all night if that was what an audience wanted and enjoyed but by throwing in a few jokes early on it was possible to tell whether my comedy was going to suit a particular audience. You learn by experience, and the bottom line is to give an audience just what it wants so that they all go home happy.

There were many bookings in my diary where I knew before I turned up just what the audience would be like, and my favourite audiences were those who just enjoyed a good mixture of music and laughs.

One such venue was the Smokey Mountain Country Music Club which had its shows at Wythall Park Hall in Wythall, Birmingham, and which I played many times in the eighties. The club was run by three of the club's members. Alan was the compere for the shows, noted for often forgetting the artiste or band's name just before he introduced them to the audience! The other two were Geoff Bishop and Ray Packham, who actually ran the club. Geoff passed away a few years ago but, at the time of writing, the club is still going strong with Ray at the helm.

Ray used to work for the Britannic Assurance Company in Moseley, Birmingham where they have a restaurant area which when it was built, with great forethought, they constructed so that it could be easily adapted into a temporary social space with a fully fitted stage. It was an ideal place to hold functions.

Ray used to hire it from time to time for an organisation which he ran the CCC. He would arrange an afternoon party for some of the less fortunate members of the locality. He had an organisation with over sixty volunteer car owners who were all prepared on an occasional basis to drive around the area picking up handicapped people, or some who were elderly and infirm bringing them to the centre for an afternoon where his helpers would provide a buffet meal for them. Ray would book an artiste to give them an hour's entertainment before the volunteer drivers delivered them all back to their homes. I just loved doing it whenever Ray invited me to entertain them. It wasn't far for me to come; Shrewsbury is only an hour's drive from there and I know just how appreciative the guests were.

Some of these people see no one for days except, maybe, the visit from Meals on Wheels. It was a really charitable and very worthy cause. You probably couldn't do it these days with all the rules and regulations in force. Each of the volunteer drivers would probably have to take out extra insurance, but it was wonderful at the time. Also political correctness would certainly not allow the organisation to be called what it was called then which seems unbelievable. The CCC stood for the 'Cripples' Car Circle!' Amazing!

It was during one of our visits to the West Country that Jean and I decided to pay a visit to an old acquaintance of ours. When I started my work at Pontin's, Hemsby, in Norfolk the general manager was a Mr Ben Lievendag from Holland. I got on really well with Ben but after a couple of years he left the company and we lost touch. Later on I heard on the grapevine that Ben was now running a pub in Devon. After a bit of investigation I discovered that his pub was The Fisherman's Cot at Bickleigh near Tiverton. We were free in the daytime so we decided to pay a call to The Fisherman's Cot as we hadn't seen Ben for a couple of years.

Ben was really pleased to see us and exclaimed, 'I can't believe it! I was only talking about you a couple of days ago.' I enquired who he was talking to about me. He said it was a friend of his who is a director of a holiday company. He could not say which holiday company, but he said that they were interested in putting on some country music festivals similar to those Pontin's were doing. He said to me, 'I told him the person he needed to speak to was Tony Best!' I thanked him and told him I would be happy to give his friend a few pointers at which he gave me his friend's business card. When I got home that week I rang his friend's number.

His friend was a director of Ladbroke Holidays and he asked me if I could spare the time to meet up with him and a couple of his colleagues at one of their venues Wallis's Holiday Centre, Cayton Bay in Scarborough which was owned by Ladbroke's. I agreed to go. Jean stayed at home, but Lynne came along with me for company. We met two directors of Ladbroke Holidays and the general manager of Wallis's, a Mr Graham Pinkney. The main question they wanted answering was, 'Just how much would it cost us to put on one of these festivals, similar to the very successful events Pontin's were running?'

Well I knew what the artistes and bands would cost them, and when I told them they were quite taken aback. They had a brief discussion and said that they certainly couldn't allocate enough money to try such a venture when they didn't know what the response would be from the paying public. Then they hit me with a very surprising suggestion. They said, 'Tony would you be interested in putting on a festival?' Straight away I replied, 'No, thank you! I'm not in that business. I'm just an entertainer travelling the country.'

They came back to me with, 'Look. We have a beautiful venue here which can take one thousand people. We can give you a very competitive rate for the villas, bungalows and caravans. We are very keen to have something like this at our centre. Ben Lievendag has recommended you as the right man to do it, and if you do think you could take it on, we'll help you.' I asked, 'How would you help me?' Then they got me! They said, 'We will help you with your advertising, and if you lose money on the first one we will cover your losses. We think you can do it!' I told them that we would give it some serious thought and get back to them as soon as possible.

By the time we got back to Shrewsbury Lynne and I had decided that this was something we just had to do. Because of the promised help from Ladbroke's if the event failed we couldn't lose. All we had to do was to convince Jean – otherwise known as the 'leader of the opposition!' She's just a very careful person.

Jean and my Mum, with her two grandchildren
Lynne and Mark.

RAF Marham table tennis team
Norfolk League Champions 1963 and 1964.
Left to right - Derek Leeming, me and Alan Pike.

"Action Man" at the table tennis table!

My band in Aden - "THE HAIRY DOGS."

In Cyprus during my table tennis tour in 1967.

"MIDNIGHT SUN" 1971-1974
Left to right- Tony Jarrett (accordion / vocals), Eric Hughes (lead guitar/ vocals), Keith Hughes (drums), Gordon Humphreys (bass guitar)

"MIDNIGHT SUN" 1971-1974

DANNY FONTANA

Sole Management
JACKIE JOHNSTON
Phone Dublin 01-506182

Supreme entertainer, Danny Fontana,
A great influence on me, and my career.

Vince Layne and me.

The Lazyacre Country Roadshow
Left to right - George Foster Tony Best, Carole Gordon, Bob Newman

Jean and me with our dear friends from Aberdeen,
Margaret and Hughie Sutherland.

Me between Nancy and Jim Kerr, great friends and
organisers of the Double K Country Music Club
at the Hotel Embassy, Dumfries. Dumfries.

Jean and me with dear friend and organiser of the
"Friends of Tony Best," Margaret, with her daughter Dawn.

CHAPTER 21

Tony Best Leisure

By the time we got back home to Shrewsbury Lynne and I were just buzzing with enthusiasm for the possibilities that this venture might put our way. With Ladbroke's fantastic offer to cover any losses on our first event we felt that we had nothing to lose, and everything to gain if things went well. They obviously had confidence in us and we felt that this could be the start of something big.

Nothing was certain though. We had never done anything like it before. In fact this was something that no private promoter had ever attempted before. Prior to us getting involved the only company which was presenting country music holiday events was Pontin's. But now it was going to be Pontin's and me! It was going to be a bit like David and Goliath, with the Goliath being Pontin's who had all the resources, and little old me as David, just dipping a toe into the water trying something for the first time. However we were prepared to give it a go. Nothing ventured nothing gained as far as Lynne and I were concerned. In fact we were really excited about the project. As I had worked on the Pontin's festivals for over four years I knew what sort of activities the guests enjoyed, and which artistes and bands were the most popular. So I did have a bit of inside knowledge to work with, and that experience gave us a good chance to keep our prospective customers happy. In addition to this, in the last few years, I had built up a great rapport with a huge number of contacts, and indeed, friends around the country whom I thought would be sure to support us in our new venture.

When Lynne and I arrived home in Shrewsbury, we told Jean all about the project. She was against the idea at first, and for a very good reason. We had just used all our savings to purchase our own house after living in council accommodation for years. She argued, 'We could lose our house. We could lose everything,' but she listened to our arguments.

Lynne and I were very persuasive, and after we had explained all the pros and cons to Jean, especially telling her about Ladbroke's offer to cover any losses if the event failed, she came round. In the end she was as enthusiastic for the project as we were. This gave us the green light to contact Cayton Bay and to tell them we were going to go ahead. Tony Best Leisure was born!

It was late 1984, and we agreed arrangements with Ladbroke's for Tony Best Leisure to present two All-Star Country Music Gala Weeks at Wallis's Holiday Centre, Cayton Bay, one in May and one in September 1985, with the important proviso that if the first one didn't work the second one would not take place.

It was only a couple of weeks after we had arranged these two events in Scarborough that I had a phone call from Southport. It was top country music DJ, Ian Ashcroft, whom I had worked with at Pontin's for four years. Ian told me that he had just played at a country music weekend at the Norbreck Castle Hotel in Blackpool. The weekend was a total flop, as not many people attended, and the event was a big disappointment. However the general manager of the hotel, Pamela Smith, spoke to Ian and told him that in her opinion something like this could work well if it was done properly. Ian suggested, 'Speak to Tony Best!' She phoned me and invited me to go and meet her for lunch one day so the following day Jean, Lynne and I drove to Blackpool and met her. She gave us a very nice lunch and showed us around the hotel.

We were very impressed with her keenness to put a country music weekend on. She told us that she realised that she had no expertise in this field, but she had a very suitable venue with a five hundred capacity ballroom in which the event could take place should we decide to do it. We could certainly see the potential, and within a couple of hours we had agreed terms with her for Tony Best Leisure to present our first country music weekend at the Norbreck Castle Hotel. The event was to take place in July 1985. Little did we know at the time that thirty years later we would be presenting the company's final event there in July 2015. We had presented well over three hundred events all over the UK and abroad in that thirty years.

I phoned Ian Ashcroft and thanked him for introducing me to the hotel, and to Pamela Smith. Unbeknown to me Ian had also left

Pontin's that year. Ian was without equal as a country music DJ and as soon as I heard he had left Pontin's I immediately invited him to join us and be TBL's country music DJ for both our events in Scarborough, and for this one in Blackpool. Ian remained as our resident DJ at all our TBL events for over ten years at home, and in Tenerife, even though he was petrified of flying.

Ian lives in Southport, and when we were arranging our final event in Blackpool for July 2015 we sent an invitation to Ian and his wife, Janet, and they joined us in Blackpool for our grand finale event back at the Norbreck Castle. It was wonderful to see them both again.

CHAPTER 22

Lazyacre at the Lord Hill

After leaving Seven Acres Club and moving to the Regency Suite of the Lord Hill Hotel we settled in very well at the new venue. We included in our programme several visiting artistes from Canada and the USA. One of these visiting American artistes was half Cherokee Indian, Marvin Rainwater (remember his big hit in the fifties *Whole Lotta Woman*? The record was No. 1 in the UK charts for three weeks in April and May 1958).

What we used to do at the club in those days was to ask members and guests to reserve tickets by putting their name on a ticket, but not pay for it until the night of the show. We did not sell the tickets in advance, but when anyone came to the admission table we would ask, 'Have you got your name on a ticket?' If they had then that was fine; if not they could come in if any spare tickets were available. Jean was on the ticket table on one particular night when a stranger came to the table. Jean asked politely, 'Have you got your name on a ticket?' The gentleman replied in a broad American accent, 'My name is on every ticket, Ma'am!' What a great reply! It was Marvin Rainwater. Once Jean realised who it was she showed him to the dressing room where his band were waiting for him. She was quite embarrassed.

In 1981 we had our first visit from an artiste who became one of our most popular visitors to Lazyacre, the great singer/songwriter Bob McKinlay with his band Dixie Fried. The band's name was taken from Bob's excellent self-written song *English Born, Dixie Fried*. Bob was a great showman a superb performer and a real bill topper.

1982 and 1983 went really well at the club. We had settled in well at the Lord Hill and things looked set fair for the future. The club's Fourth Anniversary Show featured our own Lazyacre Country Roadshow with special guest musician, 12-year-old Sarah Jory on pedal steel guitar, making her first appearance at the club. This was the first of many visits by this phenomenally talented young lady to our club. She went on to be a top name in British country music and was inducted into the British Country Music Hall of Fame on the same day that I was in 2007.

In 1983 I was singing one Friday night at the British Railway Club in Shrewsbury when some students came in. They were involved with a Charity Raft Race on the River Severn that weekend; they asked if they could go round the room selling a Charity Rag Mag., a little joke book, as part of their fund raising effort. The committee told them they could, and they sold loads at 30p each. I bought one and read it when I got it home and believe you me it was rubbish! I said to Jean, 'If I couldn't produce something better than that, I wouldn't bother!' She said, 'Well, do it then!' So I did, and in a couple of months we had the first Lazyacre Charity Fun Mag. on sale at the club and at all my gigs and festivals around the country.

We got sponsorship from local businesses to pay for the printing so the cover price of 50p was clear profit for charity. This was the start of the Lazyacre Charity Fund which over the years donated thousands of pounds to national and local charities through various activities. In the Fun Mag.'s first year we raised £2,300 for charity, and with our other fund raising activities, including a Sponsored Parachute Jump; Lazyacre was able to donate £3,500 to charity in 1983. A year later in 1984 we published Volume 2 of the Lazyacre Charity Fun Mag., once again with great success.

The club had an exceptionally strong year in 1983. There were first appearances at the club for two brilliant Scottish bands Colorado and Manson Grant and the Dynamos, a super band from South Wales, Clovis, and we were very excited to welcome a very special star guest 'Mr Guitar' Bert Weedon. You could not call Bert a country artiste though he loved country music and he had a couple of big selling albums out *16 Country Guitar Greats* and *Bert Weedon remembers Jim Reeves*. Bert was not just a great guitarist, but an excellent entertainer and a wonderful showman. Since the club was formed what we have always maintained at Lazyacre is that entertainment is the name of the game. Whenever anyone said to me that one of our artistes or bands at the club was not country I told them that the only thing I considered when booking acts for the club was, 'Would they entertain my audience?' If the answer was, 'Yes.' then they were OK by me.

Bert certainly could entertain, and on the three occasions he appeared at Lazyacre our audience just loved him.

In addition to having Bert at the club I had the great pleasure, and indeed honour, of working with him several times in theatres in different parts of the country on The Bert Weedon Show. One of these Bert Weedon Shows was particularly memorable. It was a two-night booking in Scotland with Bob, Carole and myself as the Lazyacre Roadshow, when we appeared for two nights on a Friday and Saturday in June 1985 at His Majesty's Theatre, Aberdeen as support artistes to Bert. He was absolutely brilliant. He had never appeared in Aberdeen before and he went down an absolute storm. What an entertainer, and more importantly, what a real gentleman.

I last saw Bert when he came to Shrewsbury in 2007 to do a show at the Music Hall. He was quite frail but still gave a terrific show. At the end of his show Bert spent about half an hour out front signing autographs. It was astonishing to see the number of people of pensionable age who were carrying copies of the famous Bert Weedon *Play in a Day* guitar tutor for the great man to autograph for them! When everyone had got their autographs and photos, Bert and his wife, Maggie, welcomed Jean and me to his dressing room for a quick chat. It was great to see them again and to share reminiscences.

In addition to his busy life on stage, throughout his life, Bert was an enthusiastic charity worker. His main charity was the Grand Order of Water Rats. He had been a member of this famous charitable organisation since the 1950s. Bert was very proud to be King Rat in 1992 and during the year he was King Rat the Lazyacre Charity Fund donated £2,000 to Bert for the Variety Club of Great Britain's Sunshine Coaches Appeal. This charity provides coaches for use by children with special needs. Other charities he gave great support to included Barnardos, Save the Children, the NSPCC and Bud Flanagan's Leukaemia Fund. In 2001, Bert was awarded the OBE for his services to music. This legendary entertainer passed away in April 2012 a month short of his 92nd birthday.

In July 1984 we had our very first appearance at the club of the amazing Ken Dodd. The Squire of Knotty Ash and The King of the Diddymen, call him what you wish, after this first visit Ken took a great interest in our club and went on to appear several times at Lazyacre over the years.

I had invited Ken to come to the Lord Hill to present some cheques from our Charity Fund and to do a show for us. Doddy is simply unique. After I had done my opening spot he came on stage to present the charity cheques including one for £1,000 to the Guide Dogs for the Blind Association. Then he proceeded to give us a tremendous performance, over-running our normal finishing time by over an hour, and leaving everybody breathless. It was wonderful.

I was quite surprised just how much Ken was into country music. Just thinking about it I suppose songs like *Tears*, *The River* and *Eight by Ten* could just about be called country songs while two of his biggest hit songs *Still* and *Happiness* were both written by the most prolific country songwriter of them all 'Whispering' Bill Anderson. Of course Doddy also includes in every one of his live shows the song *Special Absent Friends* written by British country artiste and songwriter Wes Cardy.

Despite Lazyacre's successes it was not all good news. I suppose that all clubs go through bad patches. Well the second half of 1984 was certainly Lazyacre's bad patch. For some reason from August onward attendances seemed to drop off to an alarming degree. We lost money on several shows. In fact we even gave serious thought to folding the club. The Lord Hill Hotel had just changed hands and had been sold to a brewery, and to add insult to injury the new manager told us that the new company's policy was going to mean some changes at the hotel. Immediately the bar prices were increased and I was informed that the room hire cost for the Regency Suite which, up to now, had been £50 per club night was going to be increased to £125 per night. With our diminishing attendances we simply could not live with this, and the hotel management wouldn't budge, so we were going to have to look for a new venue if the club was going to continue. This was a great disappointment to us because the Lord Hill as a concert venue was the perfect place for us. However with the change of ownership for some reason our members took against it. I still do not know the real reason. Maybe it was the new manager, or the bar prices, or a change of attitude. It was a mystery, and it was definitely a big disappointment.

This problem turned out to be a blessing in disguise, as we were made very welcome by the Royal Shrewsbury Hospital Sports and Social Club (The S.A.H.A. Club.) After five years at the Lord Hill we had our first show at the new venue in March 1985 and never looked back. Lazyacre attendances increased immediately. The club went from strength to strength at the hospital club and we were to be there for the next fourteen years.

CHAPTER 23

The Raymond Froggatt Saga

It was the middle of 1984 and the Lazyacre had been running for about six years when I received a telephone call from Hartley Cain known as 'H' who was the guitarist, musical director and manager of legendary singer/songwriter Raymond Froggatt. I had been fortunate enough to have seen Raymond perform on the main stage at one of Wembley's big country music festivals a couple of years previously; I was most impressed with his performance and of course with his music. H asked me whether I might be interested in booking Raymond and his band at Lazyacre sometime. I told him I would really love to have Raymond at the club but I was afraid he would be out of our price range and far too expensive for our small club.

H said that due to the fact that our shows are always on a Monday night, that Raymond and the band very rarely play on a Monday, and because they only live about twelve miles from the club in Ironbridge they would be able to do an evening for us at a very realistic fee. It really was a realistic fee too, and I was absolutely thrilled to be able to arrange a date with him when 'Froggie' and the band could play at the club.

The date we settled upon was in January 1985 and, when I announced this to our club members they were delighted at the prospect of having this superb artiste at our club, the eagerly awaited date duly came round. To support Raymond and the band I had booked that lovely duo from North Wales Iona and Andy to do the opening spot. Then we were to take a break and Froggie would do the remainder of the evening.

We had a full house, and things were going well while Iona and Andy sang for their forty-five minute opening spot. Then we had a short break before the great man took to the stage. Raymond was given a great welcome. He sang his opening number and was halfway through his second song when we had a major problem.

There were two halogen spotlights affixed to the ceiling of the room shining on the stage. A little smoke started to come from these lights, gradually getting worse until eventually there were flames. All the power was switched off and the fire brigade was called to the Lord Hill. The firemen immediately evacuated the place and we were forced to abandon the show.

Fortunately each member of the audience had been given a half of their admission ticket back so when I announced that the show could not continue I told them to keep that half-ticket and it would be valid when the show was rearranged. I spoke to Raymond and H and offered to at least pay them some expenses. They would not hear of it. They said, 'You just pay us when we come back and do the full show.' We were able to rearrange the show for a date in April. By this time the club had moved from the Lord Hill Hotel to the Royal Shrewsbury Hospital Club. The show must have been fated because just a week before the show was due Froggie was taken ill and was unable to do the show! His long awaited performance was yet again postponed.

Raymond eventually appeared at Lazyacre for the first time on Monday 17th June 1985. I am pleased to say that the evening went without a hitch, and he gave us a fantastic show singing many of his songs from my favourite Froggie album *Southern Fried Frog* which I had bought at Wembley a couple of years previously. Raymond also demonstrated his versatility by singing his hit song *Red Balloon* in French and another song he had written and recorded *Roly* in German!

Since this long awaited first appearance of Froggie at the club this charismatic performer has appeared here every year, sometimes twice in a year, since then, collecting five Lazyacre awards along the way. He has remained a major figure on the British country music scene ever since. He was inducted into the British Country Music Hall of Fame in 2008.

A few things you may not have known about Raymond Froggatt:

Raymond was born in Birmingham on 13th November 1941;

He has made over forty singles and numerous albums;

His first stage name was Steve Newman, later 'The Monopoly' then 'Frog and the Tadpoles' before going back to his real name Raymond Froggatt;

His hit song *Red Balloon* sold over five million copies worldwide and was recorded by 16 different artistes and the Dave Clark Five took it up to No. 7 in the charts;

Another of his songs *Big Ship* was recorded by Cliff Richard who took it to No. 8 in the charts in 1969;

His autobiography was released in 1992 telling stories of his early days in the music business. It is called *Raymond Who?* and is still available;

Froggie spent five months in Memphis, Tennessee making an album with The Isaac Hayes Band called *The Million Dollar Album*, which was never released.

CHAPTER 24

A Very Important Year

1985 was a very important year for me. After the launch of Tony Best Leisure at the back end of the previous year this was the year when we were going to present our first three events. Jean, Lynne and I had great hopes for the new company, but the whole future of the company probably depended solely on the success or failure of these three events. So it could probably be called a make or break year.

Also although Lazyacre was simply my hobby after the problems of the club at the end of 1984 we were more or less having a relaunch of the club at a new venue, and we didn't know how that was going to go. We had every hope that our change of venue for the club would have the desired effect but nothing was certain. It was a worry.

At the same time I could not afford to neglect my core business, which was travelling around the country entertaining people at clubs, theatres and festivals. This was my only steady source of income, and if the TBL promotions failed or if the country music club started losing money again it could have been a drain on my limited resources. So life was quite uncertain at the time, and it meant putting a great effort into all three of these activities.

My first priority was to keep the diary full, but before I even got started on that I had an exceptional piece of good luck. As I had advertised the Tony Best Leisure events at Scarborough and Blackpool it came to the notice of Pontin's Holiday Village at Sand Bay, just outside Weston-super-Mare. They knew me well from my previous involvement with Pontin's, and invited me to present two weekends at their lovely venue on the Somerset coast in the November of that year. They had previously been presenting these events themselves, but they wanted an outside promoter to take them over. Suddenly it was no longer just three TBL events in the diary for 1985; it was five including the two at Sand Bay which were already quite well established. That gave us events in three different parts of the country

North Yorkshire, Lancashire and Somerset. TBL was moving in the right direction!

Then I set to work making sure my diary was in a healthy state. Bob and Carole were now together as a couple, and were an integral part of the Roxon Roadshow, an ambitious all British touring show featuring up to nine singers and musicians which became extremely popular on the British country music scene. This meant they were not available to appear on a couple of tours of Scotland which had been pencilled in for the Lazyacre Roadshow.

I still had all the contacts in Scotland, and they were all very keen for me to bring our show to tour there. If I wasn't able arrange something it meant I was going to be left with two fourteen day gaps in my diary with no work. In order to fulfil the first of the year's tours there in May I looked for a replacement to take Bob and Carole's place. I approached the North Wales based duo Iona and Andy whom I had worked with on a couple of occasions. They fancied doing the tour but there was a problem: Iona had a full time job. She was a teacher in a school in a little village in Snowdonia. Fortunately the head teacher gave Iona two weeks unpaid holiday which meant they were able to do the tour with me. The duo had worked local clubs on a semi-pro level for a few years, but Iona's full time job meant they could only travel any distance in the school holidays. We had a very successful time in Scotland, and when we returned after the tour they made a decision to go full time. Iona gave in her notice and left teaching, and Iona and Andy became a professional act on the music scene. They never looked back.

To give myself time I cancelled the Scottish tour which had been pencilled in for October, and replaced it with two one week tours there in the August and November. The first one was with a Telford based country band, 'Silver City' and the later one was with an excellent country band I had met at Pontin's 'Burnt Ash'.

This did not mean the end of my association with Bob and Carole. We still played as the Lazyacre Roadshow on short tours around England, and on special one night stands. Throughout the years of touring together with the Roadshow the relationship between Bob, Carole and I grew very strong. We all enjoyed each other's company. We laughed at the same things, had a lot of banter and mickey taking with each other, and on stage together we just clicked. Though I have worked with hundreds of artistes during my career there are none I have had the same rapport with as Bob and Carole. The only one who came near to it was my very good friend the late Keith Manifold.

Iona and Andy and I worked together quite often after their first tour with me, including further very enjoyable tours north of the border. My diary for the year filled up with short tours of country music clubs in Yorkshire, Devon, the Bristol area and South Wales for an agent in Penarth, Len Lewis. The work from Len was a nice bonus for me because the shows I did for him were all in the Barry and Cardiff area which meant we could stay with my sister Peg in Rhoose, the village where I went to school. Len used to give me about three long weekends a year and this way I was able to keep regular contact with my family.

I remember on one of these weekends we drove down on the Friday leaving home about eleven. Before we left I had rung Ken Dodd because we were arranging a date for him to come and appear at Lazyacre again. Ken said, 'I'll have to ring you back in an hour, as I am just going out.' I said, 'I won't be here later because I am driving down to South Wales.' I gave him my sister's phone number and asked him to ring me anytime after about four knowing we'd be there by then. When we were there and the phone rang Peggy answered it. The voice said, 'Is Tony there please?' Peg said, 'Yes, who's speaking please?' She nearly collapsed when the voice said, 'Ken Dodd here!' She rushed in to me in the front room and said breathlessly, 'It's Ken Dodd! It's Ken Dodd! I've just spoken to Ken Dodd! I can't get over it, I've just spoken to Ken Dodd!' I must explain, my sister had led a very sheltered life and this was the highlight of her year if not her life! I am pretty sure that within a couple of weeks everyone in the village of Rhoose had been told that Peg had spoken to Doddy!

I had a terrific weekend at the Harlow Festival in Essex. This was a free festival put on by Harlow Council, and featured some top artistes and bands. I shared the compere duties with my old pal, Vic Woodhouse, who lived locally. It was an outdoor event in the town park. It became an annual event and Vic and I compered it for a few years; it was a good one. I was also booked to compere and entertain at a Country Music Festival in North Wales, at Presthaven Sands, near

Prestatyn, an event put on by Haven Holidays. Add to these shows about a dozen evenings with the Lazyacre Roadshow, the Scottish tours and now five TBL events and you can see that the diary was very healthy and I was kept pretty busy.

To cut down on the driving I normally tried to get two or three dates together in an area, but I did take a one-off booking at a country music club in a place called Martletwy, Pembrokeshire in South West Wales. It was 29th June. My drummer George came with me. It was about 130 miles so we left home about lunchtime to be there in good time. We just could not believe it. We went via Hereford and the Heads of the Valleys road down to Carmarthen and on to Martletwy. From start to finish of the journey the roads were totally deserted. We just didn't see a soul. It was only when we arrived at the venue that someone mentioned 'the wedding'. We realised that it was the day of the wedding of Prince Charles and Lady Diana Spencer. Everyone must have been indoors watching it on TV. No wonder we had a good run down on the roads!

CHAPTER 25

Cayton Bay – a Winner

As soon as we had made arrangements to present the two festival weeks at Cayton Bay we got down to booking our entertainment for the week. The Wallis's Holiday Centre, later known as 'Cayton Bay Holiday Village' under the banner of Haven Holidays, was in a delightful cliff top location just four miles from Scarborough's town centre. Our entertainment venue for the week within the centre was called The Rendezvous, a superb complex with two bars and a snack bar, a concert room with a huge stage and large dance floor. The concert hall had a capacity for about one thousand guests. For comfort we limited it to eight hundred. At the rear of the room was a wide reception corridor area with room for trade stalls and artistes' merchandise stands. In that reception area we had our own table with information on future events. It was a perfect venue for our purpose. Now we needed to book the artistes.

It was of paramount importance to have the right resident team of entertainers. I needed a resident band, a resident duo and a resident country music DJ. Bob Newman and Carole Gordon were our obvious choice as one of the resident acts because they were top quality. They could fill in wherever and whenever they were needed, and having them there meant we would have the opportunity to do a couple of Lazyacre Roadshow spots sometime during the week.

The resident band position was also very easy to fill because my first choice for this position told me they were available. We chose a brilliant band for the job in Essex based Hickory Lake. This was an excellent band fronted by my old pal, Vic Woodhouse, and it featured Lindsey St John, with ace pedal steel guitar player Ray Kedge. Ray now plays alongside his son in a country duo called Stonecold Country. Vic was also able to share the compere duties with me through the week, and he continued in this role for several years as my joint compere on all our TBL events in the late 1980s and early 1990s.

A great character who had a massively popular radio programme on BBC Essex. When Vic retired the radio programme was taken over, and its popularity is maintained by Steve Cherelle.

I had already asked Ian Ashcroft to be our resident country music DJ. He was by far the best in the business at that job; he too became a very important part of the TBL resident entertainments team at our events.

We introduced a very popular activity, Square Dancing, into our programme. We had an hour long session every morning just before our lunchtime show, and again in the early evening, running up to the start of our evening entertainment. For our first event we were lucky enough to get top caller Tone Howard from Suffolk. Tone did a great job for us but work commitments prevented him from becoming our regular caller. However he did us a favour by introducing us to a Yorkshireman, Ray Godfrey, who had been living (and calling) in the USA for over ten years. Ray became a valuable member of our team and was with us for many years.

With the resident team sorted we then proceeded to book the remainder of our entertainment for the week, choosing many of the most popular artistes and bands on the British country music scene at that time. Acts were booked for the evening and lunchtime shows, and even for late night singalongs in the upstairs bar.

We also arranged a number of fun events to take place during the week including a talent contest, a fancy dress competition and games competitions. The plan was to keep our guests occupied in the daytime as well as giving them the best of entertainment in the evenings and lunchtimes.

Finally we invited three attractive trade stands to set up at the back of the hall. We invited John and Janet Lang (JJ Records and Tapes) of Berkhamsted, in Hertfordshire to be our record stand. We had two western gear stands in Dave and Jean Banting, who owned a westernwear shop in Blackpool, and June Pearson (The Gambler Western Gear) from Lincolnshire who was well known at country festivals. These stalls were all very colourful and helped to give the place atmosphere even before anyone entered the room. We made every effort to ensure that our guests had a country music holiday to remember.

Despite the confidence we had in our entertainment programme and in our ability to run a successful event you just never know until the bookings come in whether it is going to work or not. I was well known from my travelling around the country, and from my four years at Pontin's, but this venture was still a massive gamble.

As soon as we had all the details of our programme arranged we advertised the holiday in the country music press. Being on the road most of the time enabled me to spread the word by carrying advertising leaflets to every venue I played at all over the country. We also built up an extensive mailing list of people who had expressed interest in what we were doing. We sent flyers to everyone in the Friends of Tony Best Club, to all members of Lazyacre and to everyone on our mailing list. We made every effort to get the word out that Tony Best Leisure was in business and that our events would be happening soon.

As things transpired we need not have worried. As soon as we started advertising the bookings for our first TBL event just flooded in. Well in advance of the event we had reached our eight hundred capacity, so all that was left to do was to make sure everyone had a good time when they came to Cayton Bay!

We must have done something right because by the end of the week at our first event we had taken bookings for over four hundred guests for our next visit to Cayton Bay in September – and thank heavens we did not need to ask Ladbroke's to bail us out! We drove home from Scarborough at the end of the week thinking, 'Wow! We've got ourselves a business!'

This was borne out by the success of our second TBL event, our weekend at the Norbreck Castle Hotel, Blackpool, just seven weeks later in July. This summertime weekend in Britain's premier resort was a winner. Guests had full board for the weekend with entertainment by Scotland's Colorado and two Liverpool bands, Kenny Johnson and Northwind, and West Virginia. We also had Tony Goodacre and Johnny Marks and our resident team of Iona and Andy with DJ Ian Ashcroft. We had a full house of over four hundred guests each of whom paid just £38 for the weekend.

Two months later we had another full house at Cayton Bay, Scarborough on our second event there in the September. Just as in May eight hundred guests enjoyed a great week with another wonderful line up of entertainment including Raymond Froggatt, Kenny Johnson, Ireland's Ray Lynam and the Hillbillies, Ben Rees, Bob McKinlay, Jeannie Dee, Tony Goodacre, Mel Hague, John C. King, Lorne Gibson and Keith Manifold. Hickory Lake was once again our resident band along with DJ Ian Ashcroft.

These first three events really put Tony Best Leisure on the map and encouraged us to increase the number of events we put on in subsequent years. We had ventured into the unknown with a few tentative steps, and come out the other side with a business which was going to grow and thrive for the next thirty years.

CHAPTER 26

The Hospital Club

Lazyacre's new venue was practically tailor-made for our purposes. The club was located in the grounds of the Royal Shrewsbury Hospital at the south end of the town; it had a comfortable lounge bar, which was well patronised by the hospital staff. It also had a big concert hall which, when available, could be hired by the general public at a very reasonable rate. The club was scarcely ever used on a Monday evening so we were able to hire it for alternate Mondays for an indefinite period.

The hall had a capacity of over three hundred seated at tables. The large stage had floodlights and theatre curtains, and spotlights located on a gantry at the rear of the hall. There was a private bar in the concert hall, and one of the most popular features was that the bar prices were working men's club prices, not hotel prices. We had our own private entrance and stage door, and two dressing rooms which were each equipped with a shower and hand basin. With all of this and a very co-operative hospital club steward the club had really fallen on its feet, and we had all we needed.

1985 and 1986 were years of consolidation for Lazyacre after all our problems at the end of 1984. We had certainly found the ideal venue. Attendances at the club settled at a good level and the club was truly back in business.

Our fund raising efforts continued with our Charity Fun Mags., which were very popular all over the country, and a new one coming out each year. We also started doing a giant charity raffle at all our Tony Best Leisure events, and this helped our fund raising in a big way. TBL would donate a free holiday as a major prize while the rest of the prizes were donated by the guests. They would then buy the raffle tickets and win them back! Then the charity concerned would benefit and get the cash. A great idea!

We had first appearances at the club by some great names including Lorne Gibson, The Cotton Mill Boys, Country Company, George Moody & the Country Squires, Charlie Landsborough, Johnny Marks, Mary Duff and a touring show - The Scottish & Country Show, featuring Manson Grant & the Dynamos, Ireland's Crawford Bell, the popular Keith Manifold and accordionist, Stuart Anderson. By the end of the 1980s we were well established at the hospital club, and Lazyacre was enjoying continued success.

We had big celebrations to mark the club's tenth birthday in March 1988. It really was something to celebrate because when we started at Seven Acres Club I had no expectation of the club lasting more than a few months. So a tenth anniversary – Wow! These celebrations included a great show from pop star, but country music enthusiast, Joe Brown who appeared for us on a special show – not with The Bruvvers but with his own excellent country band. Another one of our celebration shows featured 'Ireland's Queen of Country Music' Philomena Begley together with her band Shotgun, including a new member of the band, a sixteen year old on his first trip to England, playing lead guitar and pedal steel guitar, a young man called Stephen Smyth who has gone on to great things as one of Ireland's finest and most talented entertainers in country music.

As part of our tenth birthday celebrations in the summer of that year we took our first Lazyacre coach holiday; fifty of us went to the north of Scotland. On the first day we went just as far as Blackpool, staying overnight at the Norbreck Castle Hotel, and taking in a brilliant summer show at the Grand Theatre starring Les Dawson, Frank Carson, Keith Harris and the Roly Polys. After breakfast we left for Dumfries where we stayed at the Hotel Embassy, and were guests of the Double K Country Music Club – a concert club just like our own. Next day it was onward and upward for a four day stay in the lovely city of Inverness. The holiday was a great success, and the first of many such coach holidays for Lazyacre.

I was still doing my tours of the country, including Scotland, and in 1991 I was booked to appear at and to compere the Inverness Country Music Festival. The event was held in the Inverness Indoor Bowling Centre with a great audience of well over one thousand. The young man who opened the show was unknown to me, but standing alone on the main stage with this huge audience he really impressed me.

This was the first time I had seen Curtis Magee. Curtis came from Strabane in Northern Ireland. After his show I asked him if he ever came to England and he told me he had never been to England, but would love to come over some time. A little while later I contacted him. I had managed to find him about half a dozen bookings, including an appearance at our own club – The Lazyacre. His easy listening style of country really suited our audience, and he went on to win Lazyacre's Most Popular Solo Act award eleven times in the following fifteen years!

We were still at the hospital club when Lazyacre's twentieth birthday came round. For this very special anniversary we decided to celebrate by making the first seven shows of the year a series of celebration shows to mark this milestone in the life of the club. We started straight after our Christmas break with the first of seven shows, which starred the unique Raymond Froggatt and his band and Keith and Louise Manifold. This was followed by a comedy and country special featuring the hilarious Don D. Williams and Doreen Savage, with guest artistes, Kalibre. The third of our series of seven was our awards presentation show featuring the Mandy Allen Band and Ben Rees; the club's 1997 awards were presented by a very special guest Charlie Landsborough. Charlie presented awards to Curtis Magee (solo award,) Country Company (duo award,) Texas Gun (trio award,) West Virginia (band award) and Mary Duff (Show of the Year.) Next we had a brilliant show from Ken Dodd supported by Cardy 'n' Coke. This was followed by a special country meets folk night featuring the first appearance at the club by one of this country's leading folk bands, the Houghton Weavers. The sixth of our seven celebration shows was a wartime street party (in the club), which was a super evening of fun and nostalgia with myself and Curtis Magee. Finally on our actual birthday night we had an all action show starring Country Company, The Sunset Trio, Jolene & Barry, Denis Collier, Dane Stevens and Texas Gun. It was quite a celebration for twenty years of Lazyacre.

Right up to 1995 the Lazyacre Charity Fund continued to be a great success with the publication of nine annual editions of our little Charity Fun Mag., followed by a bumper edition containing the material from all nine previous issues. Of course we also had our giant charity raffles at all the TBL events and it was always a special night at the club when a celebrity was invited to present a few thousand pounds to worthy causes.

After the great celebrations of Lazyacre's twentieth birthday the club continued in fine form right through to 1999 with good attendances at the club and everything going along fine and dandy until in September came the bombshell.

Jean and I were on one of my working holidays in Spain when we got a phone call telling us that the hospital club had been closed by the police because of some alleged licensing and accounting irregularities. When we got home from Spain neither the club steward nor any of the committee could give me any idea when, or even whether, the club would reopen.

Unfortunately we had to cancel our shows scheduled for late September and October. We did, however, manage to book the Radbrook Hall Hotel for the Tom Russell and Raymond Froggatt Shows, and the Lord Hill Hotel for Brendan Shine in November. We were obliged to leave December blank, as neither of these hotels was available.

CHAPTER 27

Life on the Road

As an entertainer the 1980s were the busiest time of my years on the road. This was the time when I was doing over 250 shows a year, mostly one night stands in country music clubs, social clubs, theatres and events as well as my residencies at Pontin's and other festivals.

Many touring artistes on the country music scene had fan clubs and when I started touring full time a Lazyacre member, who was a family friend; Margaret Jones, suggested that she would like to organise a fan club for me. I wasn't sure. I certainly didn't care for the title 'fan club'. My thinking was that fan clubs are for pop stars and not for a jobbing singer. Margaret decided she would like to call the club the Friends of Tony Best, and that is exactly what the members became. We enclosed a membership form with every record I sold and included it on the leaflets I used to put on the tables in clubs where I played, advertising my records and the forthcoming TBL events.

The FOTB Club was a great success. Margaret sent out a quarterly newsletter to all members giving reports on shows I had done and where I was due to appear in the coming months. It also gave news of my forthcoming bookings and recordings. An added bonus was that a number of members even invited Jean and I to stay with them when we were on tour in their area. We developed a number of wonderful and very long lasting friendships as a result of this, and it added greatly to the enjoyment of our life touring the country.

I have already mentioned that when I toured clubs in Scotland with the Lazyacre Roadshow we used to hire a cottage for a couple of weeks, but later on I did several tours without the show. It was just Jean and I, and my drummer, George Foster. We dropped in very lucky when we appeared in Aberdeen with country singer, Tony Goodacre.

Tony introduced us to a lovely family: Margaret and Hughie Sutherland and their sons who used to put Tony up any time he worked in the area. Margaret and Hughie came to a couple of our shows and they said that anytime we were up there they would love to have us stay with them. This was the start of a great friendship. Hughie was a proud Shetlander who drove nationwide for a big haulage firm, Shore Porters of Aberdeen. He really hit it off with our drummer George, who was a great beer drinker. But only beer, he had a great capacity for beer, ten pints was no problem, but one shot of whisky and George was away with the fairies. Hughie the Shetlander and George's mate was a whisky man and it took me all my time to prevent Hughie from giving George a wee dram before we went out to a gig.

Margaret was a very sweet and gentle lady who looked after us when we were there and it was like home from home. She had three big strapping sons and was a lovely family lady. She would travel with us to all our gigs in the area, and helped Jean look after my records. One time I was singing in Peterhead Country Music Club about thirty miles from Aberdeen. Margaret came with us, and it was when I had the Charity Joke Books on sale. In the interval Margaret said, 'We could take them around the tables and into the bar to sell them,' so Jean and Margaret went round the club selling the joke books, thinking nothing of it. Until the following day someone in Aberdeen market went up to her and said, 'Aren't you the dirty book lady?' This gentle lady was mortified, and forever after that we used to tease her by calling her 'the dirty book lady!' Margaret is a lovely lady with a wonderful family; people like Margaret and Hughie made our touring life so much easier.

The first time I sang at Fry's Social Club in Keynsham, near Bristol we met an incredible family who also became close personal friends. The club's organiser was Tony Griffiths who worked at the Fry Factory and was a correspondent for the country music newspaper *Country Music Round-Up*. When we first met Tony and his wife Maggie they lived about ten miles away from the club in Bath. They kindly offered to put us up when we played at the Fry Club or when I was playing anywhere in their area, and they were just wonderful. We took them up on their offer many times when we were working near Bristol or Bath.

Later they moved house to Keynsham where the Fry Factory and Social Club are located. So when we stayed with them there, as we did several times, we were only about two hundred yards from the gig! I had some great times at Fry Club. I used to do their Christmas show every year and we did many nostalgic wartime street parties (in the club), and other shows during the year. Tony and Maggie always looked after us so well and we have remained good friends right up to the present day.

I really should not have started naming names because there were so many lovely people who offered such great hospitality. I am bound to leave someone out, but just one or two I simply cannot move on without acknowledging their kindness and friendship.

In Devon we would stay with Gwen and Ray Edworthy who kept a farm in Cullompton. The farm belonged to the Duchy of Cornwall (Prince Charles' estate.) Gwen and Ray would get a personalised Christmas card every year from Charles and Diana, and the couple would visit the farm from time to time. Ray and Gwen thought the world of them. One time the royal couple were due to arrive for a visit to the farm at 2pm and this was on a day when Jean and I were going to arrive as I was going to be working in their area for three nights. Gwen was hoping upon hope that we would arrive early that day so that we could meet their visitors, but for security reasons she wasn't permitted to tell us that the royals were coming. We arrived there about half an hour after Charles and Diana had left.

If I was singing in Spalding or Sutton Bridge, or anywhere around the Fens, Rob and Catherine Bettinson's farm at Whaplode was always open house for us. The farmhouse had several bedrooms and Catherine used to say to us, 'If we're not here when you arrive, you know where the key is, so let yourselves in, help yourselves to some food, and find a bedroom that isn't occupied and put your stuff in there!' Once again – home from home. Catherine and Rob also said, 'If ever you're working with other artistes, and they need a bed for the night just bring them here.' We did – several times.

On one such occasion I was doing a three day tour with a bluegrass band from Coventry The Down County Boys. On the night when we were at Sutton St Edmunds Village Hall, quite close to the farm, Jean and I had made arrangements to stay at the farm. Rob and Catherine came to the show. During the evening I learned that the band were all planning to sleep in the van and their cars that night so I spoke to Catherine and told her. She asked, 'How many are there?' I said, 'There are five in the band plus a roadie.' For anyone who doesn't know, 'roadie' is short for 'road manager', the chap who sets up and looks after all of the band's sound equipment. Catherine said to me, 'Look, I don't mind accommodating the band, but I won't take a roadie.' The look on my face must have shown I was amazed. I said, 'Why ever not, he's a lovely chap.' 'Oh!' she said, 'It's a man!' She had thought it was a groupie. The band loved that!

We got back to the farm that night and after a huge supper I told the band they would have to sing for their supper. Being an acoustic band they all got their instruments from the van - fiddle, banjo, acoustic guitar, and mandolin - and proceeded to lead a sing song into the early hours of the morning. Brilliant.

Ted and Iris Askew lived in the village of Hogsthorpe just outside Skegness. They always asked us to stay when we were in that part of the country. Ted used to organise a few shows locally in Chapel St Leonards, Hogsthorpe and Wainfleet. Ted himself would compere the shows. He wore a Stetson and called himself Texas Ted! Ted and Iris were a delightful couple and we got home cooking at its best. Ted was retired but had a smallholding on which he grew his own vegetables. Whenever we left their place we had to put our equipment on the back seat of the car because the boot was full up with fresh vegetables and a sack of potatoes. Amazing.

If we were in the Ripon area of North Yorkshire we would stay with Alan and Violet Stott, members of the Friends of Tony Best club. They would travel with us to all my shows when we stayed with them. Alan was a keen photographer and took photos of just about every artiste he's ever seen. Violet and Alan both passed away within a year of each other a couple of years ago.

A few weeks after we lost Alan I had a phone call from their daughter. She said Alan had left a huge photo album of pictures he had taken of artistes over the last thirty or forty years and she thought that I might like to have it. She also said it was far too heavy to post. So I got a couple of friends who lived nearby, and whom I was going to see later that month, to collect the photo album for me. When

I eventually received it I was staggered. It certainly was too heavy to post. It contained over five hundred beautiful photos of British country music artistes going back over many years. I have had the album on display at our club and at some of the TBL events and a glance through it immediately takes you back on a great nostalgia trip, to the time when many of these almost forgotten bands and artistes were on the scene.

I could go on with stories about Ted and Pauline Tanner in the Courtyard at Bampton in Devon, Sadie Ross in Inverness, Ronnie and Meg Watt in Elgin, Marion Ward in York, Mick and Audrey Chandler in Burbage, Wiltshire, Janet and Tony Hyke in Brigg, Humberside, Randy and Barbara Ball in Tintern in the Wye Valley, Don and Sadie Harvey in Burwell near Newmarket, Doug and Kath Backhouse in Sutton, Woodbridge in Suffolk, Albert and Madgie Ody in Wolvercote, Oxford and many more. All were lovely friends and all helped to make life on the road so much more pleasurable for us. Thank you all.

CHAPTER 28

Growth of TBL

In 1985, the year that we launched Tony Best Leisure, we presented just five events. This increased to seven events the following year – three weekends at the Norbreck Castle Hotel in Blackpool, two Gala Weeks at Cayton Bay, Scarborough, and two weekends at Pontin's, Sand Bay, Weston-super-Mare.

I had a personal setback with my health just before our July weekend in Blackpool in 1986. I had been feeling a little unwell for a time. I was feeling quite woozy and I had a constant thirst. I was drinking a lot of soft drinks and tea and coffee. Although I was not aware of it at the time these were the classic symptoms of being diabetic.

When I went to the doctor for a check up he told me that the normal reading of blood/sugar level should be between four and seven. When he checked mine it was twenty-two! After all his other examinations he advised that I should go to hospital right away. I said to him that I simply could not go to hospital because the next day I was going to Blackpool, where I had over four hundred guests depending on me being there. He asked me what was involved, and I told him I really didn't need to exert myself. I just had to be there to make sure things ran smoothly but it was very important for me to be in attendance. He telephoned a specialist at the hospital who prescribed some emergency medication to tide me over the weekend, with explicit instructions that I was not to drive and not to exert myself in any way. If I felt ill at any time I was to call an ambulance. He also gave me an appointment with the specialist on the following Monday afternoon. I thanked him and did exactly as I was told for the weekend. The event went without a hitch. Jean drove me to Blackpool and back, and on the Monday afternoon I saw the diabetes specialist, Dr Macleod, at the Royal Shrewsbury Hospital. He gave me a complete going over and I was given all the paperwork with information about the condition, together with a prescription for pills galore. I was also given a testing kit to use every morning to check my blood sugar levels.

Since then I have always kept my levels to the acceptable number and I have lived with the condition ever since without any major problems. The only thing I find is that if I have a wound or a cut of any kind it seems to take ages to heal. It is just a bit of a nuisance to get a minor scratch or a knock which takes three months to heal, but I can put up with that. About four years ago on my six-monthly visit to Dr Macleod he told me he was going to sign me off his books and that I did not need the twice a year appointment as my levels had been excellent for the last ten years. If I were to get any problems I was just to contact my GP. This had to be good news. Touch wood, things will continue in the same way.

Back to TBL, and in 1987 we added five more events making twelve in all. We kept the three venues and we added two more holiday centres. Three of the events were at Warner's Sussex Coast Holiday Village, Middleton-on-Sea, near Bognor Regis and two at Potters Holiday and Leisure Club, Hopton-on-Sea, just outside Great Yarmouth in Norfolk. Two of the weekends were in October. On the 23rd to 25th we were at Potter's in Norfolk and on the following weekend we were at Middleton-on-Sea in Sussex. We just missed the famous hurricane, or great storm of 1987 as the Met. Office prefers to call it. That happened on the 15th &16th October.

We were at Potters in Norfolk just a week after the storm. Our event was absolutely fully booked for the weekend with every chalet taken. We felt really lucky that we had just missed the hurricane by a week, but our event wasn't entirely unscathed. One block of chalets on site was made up of eleven double chalets on the ground floor level, and eleven double chalets above them on the first floor. We had forty-four guests booked into that accommodation block. The strength of the hurricane was so much that it simply lifted the upstairs chalets clean off the bottom ones leaving all twenty-two chalets uninhabitable. We only found out about this three days before we were due to arrive at Potters, so we had to make rapid arrangements to accommodate the forty-four guests. There were no chalets available on site so we had to look elsewhere. We were very fortunate that Warner's, Gunton Hall (a place we would come to know very well in later years, just six miles away), could fix us up. So we booked the accommodation there and also booked a courtesy coach which was at the disposal of these guests twenty-four hours a day over the weekend. The guests just used Gunton Hall for sleeping, and had their meals and of course, all their entertainment with us at Potters. Everyone accepted the situation really well because it was a totally unique predicament that we found ourselves in, and they knew there was no other way to deal with it. The old wartime spirit kicked in.

By the following weekend when we were at Sussex Coast – which was much closer to the where the eye of the storm had been things had settled down quite a bit. As we approached the area it was very sad to see the number of magnificent trees which had been blown down. It clearly demonstrated the immense strength of the storm. There was also quite a bit of damage to the centre. A large part of the roof of the restaurant had been blown off, but temporary repairs had been done and the centre was fine for us to go ahead with our event.

We arrived on the Thursday evening in order to be ready to meet our guests the next morning. On the Friday morning we walked down into the village of Middleton to get a bit of breakfast and we got chatting to the lady who ran the little café in the village. She told us that the storm was so fierce that her elderly mother, who lived in a house two streets away from the seafront, received a terrible shock on the night of the hurricane. A canoe was blown into the air off the beach and smashed in through her bedroom window! That is power!

In 1988 and 1989 we took our number of events up to sixteen each year, with the addition of two new self-catering venues at either end of the country. The first of these was an excellent Haven holiday park Haggerston Castle Holiday Centre just a few miles from Berwick-upon-Tweed, Northumberland, and the other was Rockley Sands Holiday Park, near Poole in Dorset.

By this time the growing TBL business was taking much more of my time but I still felt that touring was very important as it kept me in close touch with fans and friends at a local level. Also it was the thing I enjoyed doing the most. You simply cannot beat the buzz that you get when you come off stage after a really great night with a live audience. I knew that if the business continued to grow, then I would have to devote more time to it in due course, but for the moment I was going to make the most of it *–Doing What I Like Doing*. (The title track of my third album!)

At one of our events at Cayton Bay I received a phone call from Tenerife. It was none other than my old pal from the Ten Bel days, Don D. Williams. Don told me that he and Doreen were now resident entertainers in a large hotel on the island of Tenerife; and they thought it would be an ideal place for me to put on a country music holiday. Don said 'You've got to get yourself out here to see the place!' We loved Tenerife so Jean and I certainly did not need much persuading, and within weeks we were out there viewing the Hotel Punta del Rey, Las Caletillas in Tenerife.

The hotel was all that Don and Doreen had built it up to be. The rooms were beautiful, the food was excellent and it had a large concert room, which could be ours exclusively for an event, should we decide to try one. The Hotel Punta del Rey was one of a group of hotels owned by Hoteles Catalonia, a company based in Barcelona. Their sales representative was a charming lady, Sharon Smith, who would negotiate rates for our possible group booking.

It was a comfortable negotiation and we soon reached an agreement for us to present our very first Sunshine Country Music Holiday. We took with us a terrific team of resident entertainers including that popular duo from mid Wales, Country Company, The Lindsey St John Band, Scotland's Jolene & Barry, Dave Sheriff, The Haley Sisters and Keith Manifold. Also joining the team for the week would be the hotel's resident entertainers Don D. Williams and Doreen Savage.

This was the first of many sunshine holidays we presented at this excellent hotel and it was an unreserved success with 250 guests having the time of their lives. It was so successful that we immediately arranged a repeat event in May the following year and we did the same for three more years after that. After five of these holidays in Tenerife we thought it might be the right time to offer our guests a different venue just for a change. We would still be able to have occasional ones back in Tenerife but we decided to look for somewhere in mainland Spain.

By this time Sharon Smith, who had been such a help to us on our events in Tenerife, had left Hoteles Catalonia and formed her own travel agency, The Personal Touch based at Billingshurst in

Sussex. We continued to work with Sharon at all our events abroad for the following fifteen years. She accompanied us on all our foreign holidays and she was really instrumental in helping to make them so successful. She was our travel agent, flight organiser, interpreter, and anything else we needed.

When we were looking for new venues Sharon came with us as we drove all over Spain and Portugal looking for the right hotel for an event. She even came to Cyprus with us when we searched all over Paphos and Limassol for the right hotel for our very special sunshine holiday there. She was invaluable.

During the life of TBL we presented over twenty of these sunshine holidays. After Tenerife we went to three lovely hotels in Spain including Roquetas de Mar in the Almeria region, Almunecar in the Granada region and Cambrils, near Barcelona in Catalonia. We spent a fabulous two weeks in Paphos, Cyprus, during which I celebrated my sixtieth birthday, and we found a magnificent hotel in Albufeira, Portugal. It was the Hotel Montechoro at the top of what was known as The Strip, the centre of Albufeira's night life. On each of them we took a great team of entertainers who were always resident for the whole period, enjoying the holiday along with our guests. We had many wonderful holidays to remember. In fact – they were unforgettable.

So that phone call from Don D. was the start of something big. It led to a lot of pleasure for a lot of people, ourselves included. As we moved into the nineties and had our holidays abroad as well as all our events in the UK the workload was becoming heavy.

I was still touring extensively and when TBL had been in existence for ten years I needed help. That is when I invited Lynne to become a part of Tony Best Leisure full time. Since the very beginning she had always taken a keen interest in the business, but with family commitments she just gave a bit of support when she could. Now with her family growing up she could become a full partner in our company and I was thrilled when she agreed to come into the business.

Lynne's presence allowed me to continue touring the clubs etc. without feeling that I was neglecting the business. So Jean and I were able to carry on travelling the country knowing that the business was in good hands. For the duration of the 1990s TBL presented an average of about seventeen events a year, keeping our existing venues and taking on a number of new ones.

These new venues included a delightful self-catering village belonging to Haven Holidays at Chesil Beach on the Dorset Coast, plus two luxury venues owned by Warner's - Holme Lacy House, just outside Hereford, and Bodelwyddan Castle, in North Wales, near St Asaph. We also presented events at a cliff top holiday village near Weymouth - Pontin's, Osmington Bay, and at Warner's, Alvaston Hall, near Nantwich in Cheshire, all superb venues.

On all our holidays we still did our giant charity raffles, raising thousands of pounds for worthy causes. Causes often suggested by our guests. The tickets were on sale for the duration of the event and the raffle draw at the end of each holiday became a very special part of that event. At our weekend breaks we did the draw on the Sunday morning before guests had their Sunday lunch prior to going home. On the full weeklong events, guests would be leaving on the Saturday morning so the Friday evening entertainment programme at our farewell party included the draw.

The raffle on our very first event at Cayton Bay raised no less than £554 and our second event, our Blackpool weekend, added another £360. These were the sort of figures we could look forward to raising for charity at our events, and our guests just loved it. We continued to run these charity raffles right up to 1995.

CHAPTER 29

The TBL Record Label

Throughout the nineties Tony Best Leisure was going along very nicely, and in order to give a little back to those artistes who had helped the company to succeed I decided to start my own record label. I had a few albums of my own on sale and I decided I was in a good position to help a few other artistes to record material for sale to help benefit their careers. It can be very costly for an artiste to finance the recording of an album, and for them to get albums and CD's, even cassettes (which were very popular at the time) produced. They also have to consider the cost of all the artwork and the printing costs for the sleeves. Then there are royalties to be paid to the Performing Rights Society so that songwriters get their income from the recording of their songs. It was very nice to be in a position to help.

TBL sponsored a number of albums on CD and cassette by the Haley Sisters including titles like *Sisters – Best of Friends, Cowboy's Sweethearts, Blue Moon of Kentucky, Everything That Glitters, The Best of the Haleys,* and *A Little Bit of Luck,* for which I sent them to the Nashville recording studio of producer, Mark Moseley in the USA. We also produced a live video of them recorded in Oakengates Theatre, Shropshire and filmed by the Shrewsbury based firm Video Memories.

One of TBL's most popular artistes was Essex based Dane Stevens, an excellent songwriter as well as being a fine singer. I had known Dane for many years because prior to moving to his own native Essex he used to live in Newtown, about thirty miles from where I live, and he and I were on the same pub and club circuit together for a while. We produced three albums for Dane on CD. The first two entitled *Across the Miles* and *No Other Woman,* featured all self-written material by Dane, while the third album following a number of requests from his many friends and fans contained some of his most popular cover versions of songs taken from his stage act, including the title track by the late great Roy Orbison *You Got It*! Dane also brought out a special festive cassette of favourite Christmas songs and carols, with all the proceeds going to the Roy Castle Cause for Hope charity appeal. We also produced three albums for Dave Sheriff: *One Man Band Extraordinaire*, *New Western Dance*, and *Western Dance UK*, and three for Yorkshire based artiste Denis Collier, the first one entitled *Trust Me!* and two more - *Drinking and Dreaming* and *North of the Border*.

That delightful young singer from St Helens, Donna Jay, joined the TBL label with her CD *My Kind of Music*, and two top acts from Scotland, Texas Gun and Jolene & Barry collaborated to bring out an excellent CD called *Skyline of Skye*. Finally we produced three albums on CD and cassette by that fine rockabilly trio from the Northeast, The Sunset Trio. Their albums were *Workin' On It*, *You Know You Like It*, and one called *That Was Then, This Is Now*, which was half Rock & Roll, the sort of music they had previously played 'then', and half country music, which was the kind of music they concentrated on 'now.'

Of course I incorporated my own albums into the label and, all in all, we were pleased with our very attractive catalogue. I supplied the BBC and all the local radio stations in the country with every CD on our label so that fans of the artistes could send requests to get them played on the air. As a result of this the artistes on the TBL label received a lot of airplay on local stations as well as on BBC Radio 2. Terry Wogan was great because he very often played our material. The label was another very successful string to the bow of TBL.

CHAPTER 30

The Lazyacre Charity Fund

The Lazyacre Charity Fund started in 1982 when we raised £1,000 at the club to support the Charity Festival at Kyre Park House, Tenbury Wells. Kyre Park House was a residential home owned by the Spastics Society. The house accommodated forty-eight handicapped residents and had a wonderful staff of carers led by an amazing man, Mr Ewart Morgan, who in my opinion was a saint. In actual fact Ewart was the workshops manager at the centre. That was his job, but his extra-mural voluntary efforts on behalf of the residents were legendary. He did non-stop fund raising to enable him to take groups of them on holidays, including trips to Nashville, places in Europe and all over the UK. Their love of country music prompted him to bring them to Lazyacre. They became members of the club and loved their visits to Shrewsbury. In 1983 Ewart and five other carers brought twenty of the residents on one of Go-Pontinental's County Music Weeks at their centre in Cala Mesquida, Majorca. Ewart fronted the registered charity The Handicapped Holiday Appeal Fund and Lazyacre supported the fund's activities with many donations over the years.

The ways that the Charity fundraised money were many and varied. It started with a few small fund raising raffles at the club. Then came the Lazyacre Charity Joke Books, of which we produced eight annual issues between 1983 and 1990, followed by our bumper issue which contained all the material from the eight little books plus some new stuff. The bumper issue was forty pages printed on A4 paper, which was double the previous size and it sold for £3.00. All the books were very successful and were the main source of income for the Lazyacre Charity Fund. More money was raised through sponsored slims and a couple of sponsored parachute jumps added to various sundry donations. Of course the giant charity raffles at our TBL events were an absolute winning formula, and they raised thousands of pounds for the fund.

It was with great disappointment that at the end of 1995 we were forced to close down the Lazyacre Charity Fund. I was informed by the Inland Revenue that as we were not a registered charity most of the money we had raised for the many wonderful causes over the years was subject to tax. I was presented with a tax bill for over £25,000. We appealed against the decision and my accountant and specialist lawyers fought the case for us.

They worked very hard on our behalf but all they managed to do was to get the bill reduced to just over £11,000 and this I had to pay personally. The Inland Revenue told me that the Charity Fund itself should pay the tax out of its reserves but, of course, the fund had no reserves in the bank. As all our club members were aware as soon as we had any funds in the bank we would present the cheques to whichever charity we had been raising money for. It seemed that even if they were morally wrong, they were legally correct. Our protestations cut no ice with the taxmen. I had to cut my losses and treat the £11,000 as a personal donation from me.

So the Lazyacre Charity Fund was no more, with the losers being the many charities we had been raising money for. This was very sad and most disappointing. Below is a list of the various charities which we supported over the fourteen years the fund was in existence, and which would no longer be supported by the Lazyacre Charity Fund.

The Kyre Park Handicapped Holiday Fund	£19,400
The Guide Dogs for the Blind Association	£13,350
The BBC 'Children in Need' Appeals	£12,000
Roy Castle's 'Cause for Hope' Appeal	£8,700
Leukaemia Research	£6,475
Shropshire & mid Wales Hospice	£6,000
Great Ormond Street Hospital	£4,850
The Motor Neurone Disease Society	£4,500
Royal Shrewsbury Hospital 'League of Friends'	£4,000
The Shropshire Sharks	£3,850
Elms House Residents' Comforts Fund	£2,100
The Gary Hart Leukaemia Trust	£2,000
Variety Club of Great Britain Sunshine Coaches	£2,000
P.A.C.T Ward E39 Nottingham Hospital	£1,900

The Cally Ann Gray Appeal	£1,850
The Hillsborough Disaster Appeal	£1,835
The Robert Clive School, Shrewsbury	£1,550
The Katharine Elliott School, Shrewsbury	£1,350
The Cot Death Society	£1,100
Dial-a-Ride, Nottingham	£1,000
The Ricky Sylva Appeal	£1,000
The Zeebrugge Channel Ferry Fund	£980
The West Midlands Children's Hospice Trust	£750
The Marc Wayne Appeal	£700
Royal Shrewsbury Hospital Cobalt Unit Appeal	£700

Donations between £400 and £650 totalling **£10,135**
to Meole Brace Handicapped Work Centre,
Eastgate Handicapped Centre, Sleaford,
'Safe Play for Sarah' Appeal, Hope House Children's Hospice,
The Cancer Research Campaign, Llandrindod Wells Lions Club,
Multiple Sclerosis (Great Yarmouth),
Peter Frampton Benefit Appeal, Shrewsbury CT Scanner Appeal,
St John's Ambulance Brigade, The British Diabetic Association,
Oswestry Spinal Studies Centre, Kyre Park 'Parker Bath' Fund,
Oswestry Orthopaedic Spinal Ward, A.R.M.S. (Multiple Sclerosis),
Scarborough Lifeboat Crew Fund, Gnosall Surgery Equipment,
Oswestry Orthopaedic Orlau Fund, North Staffs Nurse Education,
Zipper Club (Open Heart Patients.)

Donations between £200 and £380 totalling **£ 5,273**
to Bob McKinlay's Kevin Duffy Appeal,
Ron Dorricott Van Adaption, The British Heart Foundation,
The Bradford Fire Disaster Appeal, The Brittle Bone Society,
Oswestry Talking Newspaper, Felicity Ashdown Appeal,
Heath Houses Wheelchair Fund, P.H.A.B (via Mel Hague Appeal),
Kempsfield Hostel for the Handicapped,

The Winifred Jones Trust, Eskdale Road Adult Training Centre,
Holme Towers Hospice, Wheatlands Home, Baschurch,
Williams Day Hospital, Harlow,
Shropshire Association for Sick Children,
Arthritis Care (Birmingham), ME Group (Llandrindod Wells),
White Horse CMC Charity Fund, National Society for Epilepsy.

Donations between £100 and £179, totalling £1,871
to Donnington Guides Roof Appeal, Wellington Arthritis Council,
Shrewsbury Samaritans, WM Disabled Motorists' Club,
Shrewsbury Helping Hand Society, Winchester House, Elgin,
Jeanette Woodward Appeal, R.B. Legion Poppy Appeal,
Carlisle Handicapped Children's Fund, Notrees Home, Kintbury,
Inverurie Disabled Taxi Appeal, Oswestry Adult Training Centre,
Cancer Aid, Wakefield Dyslexic Association,
Shrewsbury Diabetic Association.

----

plus fourteen donations of less than £100 totalling   £670

A GRAND TOTAL OF £121,839

Carole Gordon & Bob Newman
receiving their Lazyacre Award from Club President,
"Griff" of Miki and Griff at Lazyacre CMC in 1984.

Stars who became great friends, Miki and Griff.

My pal Vic Woodhouse and me.
Joint comperes of the Harlow Country Music Festival.

Ken Dodd receives a cheque from Kerri Pugh, ("Miss Lazyacre") to present to one of the charities supported by the Lazyacre Charity Fund.

Ken Dodd presents a cheque for £1,000 to Mrs Dorothy Jones of the Guide Dogs for the Blind Association from the Lazyacre Charity Fund.

Receiving my "Heart of Britain" Award 1994.

Shropshire Star newspaper cutting 1994.

Mother and Father Christmas - Jean and me.

Fans and good friends, Alan and Violet Stott of Ripon.

Jean and me with our dear friends, Alice and Keith Manifold
on their superb new canal boat.

Family photo.
Left to right: Niece, Jacqueline (sister Peg's daughter,)
Grandaughter Michelle, Lynne with our grandson, Thomas,
Grandaughter Beverley, Sister Peggy, her husband, Jock, Jean and me.

Two snaps of Jean
and me...

...don't we scrub up
well?!

"The ladies in my life"
Standing L to R - Daughter Lynne, Grandaughters Michelle and Beverley,
and my wife Jean.

"TEA AT THE RITZ"
A treat given to us in 2013 by our Lazyacre friends.

CHAPTER 31

The Radbrook Hall Hotel

The Royal Shrewsbury Hospital Sports and Social Club was everything we could have wished for in a venue for Lazyacre Country Music Club. A large concert hall with a big capacity, a lovely large stage, dressing rooms, ample car parking, and last but not least, very reasonable bar prices. We were most comfortable there for over fourteen years when suddenly, at a moments notice, in September 1999 we lost it through no fault of our own.

The whisper was that either one of the committee or the club steward had forgotten to renew the club's drinks licence. They each blamed the other one! So the club had been running for a few months with no drinks licence, when the police raided it one Saturday night and closed the place down. For the committee to reopen the club they would have to re-apply for a licence, starting from scratch. This meant having checks on the plumbing and the kitchen (because they served food), and checks by the dreaded Health and Safety Executive. After the completion of all these checks, it was discovered that a massive amount of money (over £30,000) was needed to put everything in order to obtain the licence. It was the generally accepted opinion that it was most unlikely that the club was going to reopen. This opinion turned out to be correct; after standing empty for a considerable amount of time the building was eventually demolished.

Lazyacre had to find a replacement venue – and quick! We had done two shows in October 1999 in the very nice Radbrook Hall Hotel, and we had done a one-off show that November at the Lord Hill Hotel, which had been our home for nearly five years prior to moving to the hospital club. So both of these hotels was a possibility. They both suited our purpose, although neither had the capacity of the hospital club – or the cheap bar prices! I went ahead and made appointments with the managers of both hotels.

The manager of the Lord Hill made it quite plain he did not want us there. He said, 'Your people don't drink enough! Because of this,' he went on to say, 'the hire charge for the function room would be sky high.' He gave me a figure which was out of the question. So the Lord Hill Hotel was definitely a No No! I did not know who the manager of the Radbrook Hall was, but when I went for our appointment it was a manageress, Jill Ellis. We knew her well and she knew the Lazyacre very well because she had been a barmaid at the Lord Hill when we were there fourteen years previously. Jill was very keen to have us at the Radbrook. After all we were offering to bring nearly two hundred people on a Monday evening every fortnight. That has to be good business and Jill understood this. She said that she would charge us a nominal hire fee for the room because she would offer hot and cold snacks for sale, as well as having the bar receipts.

We readily accepted her terms and in January 2000 we presented our first clubnight in Lazyacre's new home, the Porthill Suite of the Radbrook Hall Hotel. We certainly could not have asked for better co-operation than we got from Jill and her team. We were made very welcome; the club was in a comfortable new environment and we were in business again.

It took us a little while to adjust to the new venue as it was totally different to the huge hall at the hospital club. But though we lost some capacity the new function room had its advantages. It had a great atmosphere. The audience was seated right up to the stage so it was much more intimate. The artistes loved it and so did the members. Although the bar prices were higher than we were used to, the hotel served excellent hot and cold meals and snacks at very reasonable prices. So, swings and roundabouts, our new venue was fine.

We opened in the Porthill Suite of the Radbrook Hall Hotel on the 10th January 2000 with the tremendously popular local duo, Country Company along with a band from South Wales, The Rimshots. It was a good start to what was going to be just over six years in this very pleasant venue. We would have been happy enough to stay there indefinitely but when we had been there about five years the hotel was sold to new owners. Although they were happy with us and we were happy with them about a year later they sold the hotel to a building company whose plans were to redevelop the site for housing.

In next to no time the Radbrook Hall Hotel was flattened and now it is a housing estate with seventy-odd houses and flats. This was very disappointing and we had no alternative but to accept the situation. Once again Lazyacre would have to be on the move! But where next?

CHAPTER 32

Open Heart Surgery

A problem arose in March 2005. On my birthday Jean and I went to the Grand Theatre in Wolverhampton to see a show. We parked the car in the car park and walked up to the theatre. Half way up to the theatre I got a slight chest pain and had to stop for a few minutes. Jean quizzed me, 'Have you ever had anything like this before?' I said that I had on a couple of occasions, but it is always OK after a minute or two. Then she laid down the law to me! 'You are going to the doctor first thing in the morning!' So I did.

The doctor examined me and suspected a problem, so he referred me to the hospital for an angiogram. I received notification to attend the hospital for the test within the week. Lynne and Jean both came with me because they knew how nervous I was. There were three other patients as well as me in for an angiogram that morning. The staff explained to us what would happen. We would be on a trolley whilst the procedure was carried out. There was a screen above me on the trolley, and they told me that if I wanted to I could watch it all on the screen as it was being done. I said, 'No, thank you!' I just wanted to close my eyes until it was all over. I cannot stand anything like that. I am so squeamish that I do not even want to talk about it!

After it was over all four of us patients had to wait in a ward until the results came through. We were told that whatever the problem was it could be treated in different ways. Firstly, it could just need medication – tablets presumably, or we might need angioplasty, which is a simple procedure whereby they insert one or more stents into the artery. The final option is a full heart bypass operation, which means open heart surgery. Of course we were all hoping it would be a tablet job!

When the verdict finally came, my worst fears were realised; I was told I would need a full heart bypass operation. I dreaded it. I had already decided I would have no chance of coming through an operation like that. After all I was overweight. I was diabetic. As far as I was concerned, I was a goner.

A week or so later I had my first meeting in Shrewsbury hospital with the surgeon, a Mr Levene, from the specialist hospital in Stoke-on-Trent where the operation would take place. I told him of my fears, and that I thought I had no chance. He reassured me as best he could. First of all, he said, 'I've successfully operated on much larger patients than you!' He went on to say, 'Although you are diabetic, all your other readings are perfect. You have never smoked, and apart from the problem we are going to deal with you are in good health. I'll bring you through this, so don't worry.' He told me that he can normally discharge a patient within five to seven days of the operation, but it may be ten to twelve days in my case. He assured me that I would not have a problem.

The operation was scheduled for about six weeks later, and I asked him, 'If I lose some weight in the next six weeks would that give me more chance of coming through this?' He said that it was not necessary, but if I did lose some weight it could do nothing but good. So there and then I decided I had to do it. I lost a stone and a half in those six weeks.

We were at an event at Bracklesham Bay a couple of weeks before my operation; I was sitting in the lounge talking to my pal Keith Manifold when one of the guests, a dear little elderly lady said to me, 'Oh, I say, you've lost some weight.' I did not like talking about the operation as the thought of it filled me with horror, but I said, 'Yes. I'm having an operation shortly, so I thought I should lose some weight.' 'A very good idea,' she replied, 'Not so much flesh for them to cut through!' I nearly died right there and then, and we practically had to pick Keith up from the floor he was laughing so much.

I had to visit Mr Levene in Stoke a few days before the operation for what they call a pre-med. This is when they tell you everything they are going to do in detail and you have to sign a consent form to allow them to do it. I asked him if I could just sign the form without him giving me all the gory details, and he said that I could not. So I had to live through it all before he even did anything.

True to his word Mr Levene brought me through the operation which went exceptionally well. After this operation at Stoke they insist that before a patient can be discharged he has to complete 'the marathon'. The marathon was a two hundred metre walk through the corridors of the hospital accompanied by a nurse, down two flights of stairs, back up those stairs, then back two hundred metres to the ward – and that is a half-marathon; you have to do it again straight away to complete the marathon. You then get a badge saying 'I've completed the marathon', and if all else is in order you can be discharged.

On the fourth day after my operation I did a half-marathon, and on the fifth morning I did the full marathon. As I was just getting back to the ward after my second lap Mr Levene was coming out of the ward. He asked how I felt, and had I done the marathon. I told him I felt fine and that I had just completed the marathon. He said, 'I've just been to the ward and checked all the numbers. You can go home today.' I could not believe it. I was expecting ten to twelve days in hospital and I was leaving on the fifth day. Brilliant.

Obviously I cannot speak highly enough of the surgeon and the team at the hospital in Stoke. Their work gave me a completely new lease of life. That is just one of the reasons you will never ever hear me complain about the NHS.

When I got home from the hospital I had to take things easy for a while. The hospital had equipped me with a huge corset which I had to wear for six weeks just to keep everything together. It was very tight and I was allowed to take it off for half an hour each day just to give me a breather. It was uncomfortable but necessary, and I slept sitting up for those six weeks. It obviously did the job. On the advice of the hospital from about the third day home I did a little walking, going a little further each day and within a very short time I felt better than I had for a long time.

I had the operation at the end of August, and I had to spend about four months convalescing. It was just as well that I was no longer on the road because there was no possible way I could have strapped my accordion on. I had to miss one of our TBL events at Bracklesham Bay as I was still wearing my corset! It was early in 2006 before I was able to do a day's work in the office, but I only missed two Lazyacre shows.

CHAPTER 33

Back Home to the Lord Hill

It was just a few weeks after my convalescence that we got the news that Radbrook Hall Hotel was being demolished for building development and we would have to find a new home for Lazyacre. This was not going to be easy. I asked members of the club to come up with ideas as to where we could take the club. Hotels with a function room of the size we required were few and far between in the Shrewsbury area; we were getting suggestions of venues like village halls where guests would have to bring their own drinks which would not have been very satisfactory.

The Lord Hill Hotel was by far the best option, but after the scathing remarks of the manager the last time we had to move I thought we would have no chance of being accepted there. But when I enquired things had changed, and the news was good.

The Lord Hill was now under new ownership and the whole management team had been replaced. I made an appointment with the new owners and their hotel manager. The people who had purchased the hotel were a lovely couple from Scotland, Raymond and Vera Proctor, and their general manager was a local man from near Welshpool, Mark Chapman. During our meeting I told them about the previous manager's reservations about our group. I put them in the picture that the club had been running successfully for twenty-eight years, and I told them the reason why we had to move away in 1985. To cut a long story short they welcomed us with open arms.

We already knew from our time at the hotel in the early eighties that the function room was perfect, and the only reason we left in 1985 was because the new ownership at the time, a brewery, had priced us out of it. As I write this it is now close to ten years since we moved back to the Lord Hill. I can honestly say that the last ten years has probably been the most successful period in the whole life of Lazyacre.

Membership numbers have increased to over five hundred and attendances on clubnights have been terrific. The days have gone when members and guests could just turn up on spec for a show. We have had to make every show a ticket show. This has been necessary because the club's popularity was getting to the stage when we were turning people away at the door, and if you turn someone away it is very unlikely they are going to come again. So we have made every show a ticket show and it works very well. The club is thriving with wonderful support from the members, and it has a really lively feel to it.

This success has coincided with the growing popularity over here of the top Irish bands and artistes. Back in the 80s and 90s when we were at the hospital club we used to have an occasional visit from a few top Irish artistes like Brendan Shine, T.R. Dallas, Ann Breen, Mary Duff and Dominic Kirwan, all of whom still come and play at the club. But in recent years the number of fine Irish bands and artistes coming to England to work has snowballed. The vast majority of them are just excellent. They take the trouble to dress smartly for the stage and put a great effort into their performances. Acts who are now regular visitors to Lazyacre include Shaun Loughrey, Mick Flavin, Declan Nerney, Paddy O'Brien, Shawn Cuddy, John McNicholl and Stephen Smyth and their bands, plus Frank McCaffrey, Curtis Magee, Kenny Paul, The Indians and several more who are hugely popular at the club.

In addition to our regular fortnightly clubnights every other Monday we also put on a number of special events for our members throughout the year. We get excellent support for these extra events. Every November about a hundred members come away with us to Blackpool for a great festive Turkey 'n' Tinsel weekend. The break runs from Friday to Monday in the superb Park House Hotel on the promenade. We also take trips to the theatre and twice a year about eighty members come to Monmore Green Greyhound Stadium in Wolverhampton for a 'night at the dogs' with a three course meal and an exciting evening's entertainment included.

We have taken many coach parties of members to various theatres including Venue Cymru in Llandudno, The Pavilion Theatre in Rhyl, Lichfield Garrick Theatre, The Floral Pavilion in New Brighton,

Birmingham Hippodrome and Wolverhampton Grand Theatre. The shows we have seen include productions right across the board including music, comedy and an annual visit to a pantomime, for which we always book over a hundred seats.

Yes the club has gone from strength to strength in recent years and long may it continue.

CHAPTER 34

Retirement

During the time that Lazyacre was at Radbrook Hall Hotel I continued to be heavily involved in the running of the TBL business, with Lynne sharing the office work with me and Jean lending her support. Jean and I also continued to tour all over the country. We still loved doing this because it kept us in touch with the many wonderful friends we had made during our years on the road. Jean was not just company on our travels. We shared all the driving - Jean was my night driver! Fortunately my services were still in demand and the diary still looked very healthy.

It was in late 2004 when I made a big mistake. I decided it might be time to cut back a bit and I decided to semi-retire. After all I was coming up to seventy and most working people have retired by that age. My plan was to cut down on the travelling and just take bookings at places where I really enjoyed playing. For years I had accepted anything and everything that was offered in an effort to keep the diary full, and to ensure that we had a decent income. But there are some gigs which are just a pleasure to play; I thought I could still earn a reasonable income if I concentrated on those shows to the exclusion of the others.

That was my mistake. I started telling people I had retired, while still accepting the special bookings. Imagine getting an enquiry for a return booking at a club, refusing it because you have retired, only to be told, 'Well you've taken a booking for such and such a club, why won't you do mine? You cannot say, 'It's because yours is a rubbish club,' or 'because I don't enjoy playing at your place!'

So I talked it over with Jean and we decided we had to have a change of plan. We would retire from touring in March 2005, on my 69th birthday, and take no bookings after that – not even the nice ones! Although I did make one exception. That was when Bob, Carole and I did one final Lazyacre Country Roadshow booking at the Queens Theatre, Hornchurch in Essex. This theatre really was one of our favourite places to play and we had a wonderful celebration evening there. I say I was retired but of course Tony Best Leisure was still going strong, and I did get the chance to sing a few songs at our holiday events so I kept my hand in. 2005 was the year when I really did retire from touring. I also retired from actually running Tony Best Leisure and allowed our daughter Lynne to take over the reins, with Jean and me in the background giving her our support.

Lynne took over the running of our company and she was quite brilliant at it. The company continued to thrive under her stewardship. TBL was soon registered as a limited company with Lynne in place as Managing Director, but behind the scenes we continued working together as a partnership. Jean and I still attended every event; I was host and compere at all the events but Lynne was the boss, and I liked it that way. She has a great talent for putting guests at ease and for looking after guests who have any sort of problem. The company was in good hands.

So really I was still only semi-retired, but it suited me fine. There was no more travelling thousands of miles on ever-increasing busy roads with never ending roadworks at every corner. But I still had the pleasure of seeing guests we had come to know over the years, many who had become personal friends. So I had the best of both worlds, and I still had my very enjoyable hobby, the Lazyacre, which was ongoing and flourishing. It was going to be another ten years before I retired completely.

Jean and I loved attending the events. I enjoyed being the compere of the shows and I enjoyed having the occasional chance to sing a few songs on stage for old time's sake.

Between attending Lynne's events Jean and I had more time to do the things we enjoyed. About twice a year we would take the train to London and spend three or four days there, taking in two or three West End shows. I have always loved the theatre and Jean also enjoys it very much, especially musicals. Some of our favourites over the years were Barnum, with Michael Crawford, Billy Elliott, *Hairspray* with Michael Ball, Mamma Mia, Buddy, *Les Miserables*, Joseph, with Phillip Schofield. *We Will Rock You*, *The Producers*, (which we saw twice) *Starlight Express* and *Jersey Boys*, which we have seen four times as it is our real favourite. We enjoyed Tommy Steele in *Singing in the Rain* and in his own life story production *The Tommy Steele Show*, and we enjoyed plays like *An Inspector Calls* and *The Mousetrap*, which we saw twice with a ten year gap in between, and we still couldn't remember whodunnit!

Other things which we were able to do were to pay visits to my family in Barry in South Wales. This is always a terrific nostalgia trip for me. I cannot visit my folks in Barry without driving down into the Vale of Glamorgan and through my home village, Aberthaw, pointing out to Jean all the places I used to play as a kid. By now she can tell me all those places herself she has heard it so often, but a visit there brings it all back to me and I love it.

We also love visits to the North Wales coast, particularly to one of our favourite resorts, Llandudno. We still visit the Isle of Anglesey where we spent eight happy years, just for old time's sake. Two of my old band Midnight Sun live there so we visit them. The fourth member of the band, our drummer Keith, passed away a few years ago. Our daughter Lynne also often visits Anglesey because her best friend since schooldays in Amlwch (another Lynne) still lives there and they have remained firm friends for over forty-five years, and although they live 120 miles apart they still see each other several times a year, often meeting halfway in Llandudno where they both worked in a hotel for a summer season when they left school.

So we have plenty to do to fill our time, and it is a pleasure not to be racing around the country on a tight schedule on today's roads. In fact it is a pleasure not to be driving at all on today's roads. If we travel any distance Lynne drives us or we just take the train.

CHAPTER 35

Another Setback

With my diabetes under control and with my good recovery from my heart bypass my general health remained very stable. However, at the beginning of 2014 I had another minor setback health-wise. It was a Monday evening and we were actually at Lazyacre. We had just had the interval and I had introduced our artiste for the start of the second half of the evening. I went back to my ticket table in the reception area. One of our members came along and bought two of my CD's; he asked me to autograph them for his wife, whose birthday it was that evening. I was horrified to find I could not write my name. My hand seemed to feel like it belonged to someone else. I could not write. Jean was not with us at the club that evening. She had stayed at home with a heavy cold. I called Lynne over, and she looked at me and noticed that my face was down on one side. By now I could hardly talk. She dialled 999 and within just a few minutes an ambulance arrived with a couple of paramedics. The paramedics carried out all sorts of tests on me and told me I had suffered what they call a TIA or mini-stroke. Within less than half an hour I felt absolutely fine again. They told me that if I wished they would take me to hospital, but suggested that I did not really need to go there as they had done all the necessary tests and the hospital would only do all those same tests again. I could go home as long as someone was going to be with me.

They said that I may never have another one of these mini-strokes. On the other hand they said it was quite possible that I would have another one, or even a full blown stroke. They told me to just take things easy for a few days. Lynne took me home and had to put Jean in the picture as to what had happened. I had a little supper and went to bed. Lynne stayed the night as she wanted to be on hand if I had any problems during the night. I went to the bathroom a couple of times in the night; Lynne was wide awake, I think she must have stayed awake all night. Each time I passed her room to go to the bathroom she called out, 'Are you OK, Dad?' Each time I replied that I was.

Then at six in the morning I certainly was not OK. I was numb all over. I could not speak but somehow I said, 'I've got a problem.' Lynne phoned the ambulance and within ten minutes I was on my way to the Princess Royal Hospital, Telford where they have a dedicated stroke unit. Jean and Lynne followed the ambulance in our car and stayed with me all day.

When we arrived in the ambulance at the doors of the hospital there was a surgeon, another doctor and a stroke nurse waiting for me. I was on a trolley in no time, being wired up to all sorts of bits of apparatus. In less than an hour I had received an ultrasound scan, a CT scan, an MRI scan, a neck scan and Lord knows what else. I had had blood tests, blood pressure tests, all sorts of tests, and the doctors and staff were brilliant.

They gave me some lunch and put me in one of their stroke wards to rest for a while until they sorted out some medication for me. When it got to about five in the afternoon I felt pretty well. I know my right hand and arm were pretty useless and my speech was very poor but in myself I felt fine. I was certainly not nearly as bad as the other occupants of that stroke ward. I was dreading the doctors coming to the ward and saying that I would have to be admitted to hospital for a while.

When the main doctor arrived at the ward, I just asked if there was any reason I could not go home. She said that they had sorted out my medication and as long as there was someone at home who could look after me I did not need to remain in hospital. I could have jumped for joy. They put me in a wheelchair to get me to the front door and helped me into our car, which had been parked at the hospital all day after Jean and Lynne had followed the ambulance in the morning. They then drove me home to Shrewsbury. Lynne decided to stay at ours for a few days (the few days turned out to be a few weeks) just to make sure everything was alright, so I had two wonderful Florence Nightingales looking after me! When you hear so many people complain about the National Health Service, this next piece is unbelievable.

At 9am the next morning our front door bell rang. At the door was a young man who introduced himself as Neil, the leader of a new team of nurses and therapists from the Royal Shrewsbury Hospital's Stroke Support Team. The purpose of this newly formed unit is to support stroke victims for the first six weeks after a stroke. There were about six members of the team and for six weeks at least one of the team would visit me at home each day to give advice and information, speech therapy, physiotherapy, balance therapy, handwriting, in fact everything to help get me back to normal as quickly as possible. It was a marvellous service. Neil, the team leader, was about thirty, all of his team were youngsters but obviously well qualified. Their dedication was quite amazing and I am convinced it is down to the speed of the ambulance attendance, the rapid work of the stroke unit in Telford, and the amazing efforts of Neil's team that I came out of a stroke as quickly and as well I did. It was nothing short of Five Star Service and I can't thank them enough.

At the time of writing this it is about eighteen months since I had the stroke and I have come through it very well. I have fully recovered the use of my right hand and arm which were useless for a couple of months but the physio from Neil's team did wonders for that problem. My balance is still a bit iffy, so I am very careful. I notice it most when I am standing on stage introducing our shows at Lazyacre, and my speaking voice is not yet back to normal, but I notice it more than anyone who is listening to me. When I see or hear of others who have had a stroke, and suffered much more severely than I have, I just thank my lucky stars for the prompt actions of the emergency services and the NHS. I consider myself one of the lucky ones.

CHAPTER 36

TBL – The Later Years

When Lynne took over the management and running of our TBL business in 2005 she had already been working with me for ten years so she was well versed in what was required to promote our events. She took to the management role like a duck to water and the business continued to thrive the way it always had.

I left the running of the business completely to Lynne. The only input from me was if she asked me to help in any way. This often happened when it was time to do the choosing of artistes and bands to appear at our events. Having done it for years I was much more conversant with the geography of where artistes were based, and which ones would work well together, than Lynne was. So she picked my brains. Once we had made up our minds just who we would like on our events Lynne took over again and booked and contracted the artistes and bands. The system worked well and I was free of all responsibility, but there if she needed me.

Of course Jean and I attended all the events and I continued to compere the shows. This was the one thing that Lynne was convinced that she could not do, although on one occasion when I was taken ill she had to, and everyone said she did it brilliantly. But it was not something she wanted to do, or enjoyed doing.

Where she did excel was in dealing with our guests, putting them at ease and making them feel wanted, which they were. She was simply excellent with people and very popular with our guests.

Our holidays abroad over the years had become more and more difficult to make viable because so many promoters were now putting these sunshine holidays on. Many artistes were holding fan club holidays abroad, and of course the Irish scene supported by the Irish country music TV channel was advertising loads of special events abroad, so it had become very difficult.

Lynne concentrated on fewer venues. Making sure that the events presented by TBL were in the best of venues with the top artistes and bands, and making sure our guests had a great time if they came on a TBL break. This was not difficult because we had been doing this for over twenty years!

About three months after I had my stroke in January 2014, I had made a pretty good recovery and I was looking forward to being able to drive again. However when I got behind the wheel I found that I had lost all my confidence, and the driving actually scared me. I left it a few days before trying again with the same result. I gave it a try three or four times but each time it was the same. On a couple of occasions I had to get Jean to take over because I was so uncomfortable. It was very strange. Driving had been second nature to me. After all I had been doing it for over fifty years, but I was hesitant and dithery, and I felt I would be dangerous on the roads. I did not want to take risks so I decided to send my driving licence back to Swansea, and quit driving altogether. Jean and Lynne are both good drivers and they were both happy to drive. I hated being a passenger at first, but now I have got used to it and it is not so bad.

Jean and I took a little time pondering what to do and eventually we decided that I should retire completely from the business. We brought Lynne into the discussion and she surprised us by saying that she really did not want to continue running the company without my help. She said that she loved running the events while they were happening, but eighty percent of her work was in between events. Sitting in the office in front of a screen doing secretarial work, and without her Mum and Dad on hand, she did not fancy it.

This was when we all had a meeting and decided that the best thing to do was to close the company down. If we were going to do this we were determined to go out of the business with a flourish. We had four of our events already booked between March and July 2015 and we decided to make these four events into special celebration events. The final one of these was the July weekend at Blackpool's Norbreck Castle Hotel, which was due to take place exactly thirty years after our very first weekend there in 1985. So we decided that this event was to be our grand finale. There were four more events scheduled for later on in the year, but we cancelled all of those so that we would be able to close the company down after our thirtieth anniversary event in Blackpool. All four of these celebration events were very successful with full houses for every one of them. We approached the final weekend at Blackpool with very mixed feelings, but it was clear to us all that we had had the very best of times over the past thirty years, and we had enjoyed every minute of it.

Our guests gave us a tremendous send off. We had some lovely letters of appreciation and literally hundreds of cards and some lovely gifts. There were a few tears shed, but it was the right thing to do and the right time to go.

CHAPTER 37

Awards

It is very gratifying to know that you have been appreciated by your audiences and that you have been considered for an award of some kind. I have been very fortunate over the years in this respect, below is a list of awards that I have picked up over the years since I turned professional in 1975.

The awards which gave me the most pleasure to receive were the ones actually voted for by the audience members themselves. These are the people who pay to come in and by doing so keep us entertainers in a job. The awards presented by organisations and committees are also very welcome, but keeping the customers happy is the name of the game and if they vote for you to receive recognition that is much more important.

Of course I was very honoured to be inducted into the British Country Music Hall of Fame in 2007. This was a real accolade for me, especially when I look at the other names who have been similarly recognised.

1978
North Staffs and South Cheshire Entertainments Federation
Comedian of the Year
Western Star Promotions
Comedian of the Year

1979
White Horse Country Music Club, Burbage, Wiltshire
Best Show of the Year (The Lazyacre Roadshow)
White Horse Country Music Club, Burbage, Wiltshire
Best Comedy Act of the Year (TB)
Lazyacre Country Music Club, Shrewsbury
Special Award from members.
North Staffs & South Cheshire Entertainments Federation
Comedian of the Year

1980
Kama Records
Top Sales Award for LP – Tony Best - By Request
White Horse Country Music Club, Burbage, Wiltshire
Best Entertainer of the Year
Wales Country Music Festival Awards
Club of the Year (Lazyacre CMC)
The Big D Country Music Club
Best Band of the Year (The Lazyacre Roadshow)

1981
The Log Cabin CMC, Mastin Moor
Artiste of the Year
Wales Country Music Festival Awards
Supreme Award (Lazyacre CMC)

1982
The End of the Trail CMC, Worcester
Solo Artiste of the Year

1983
Smokey Mountain C&W Club, Wythall, Birmingham
Solo Artiste of the Year
The End of the Trail CMC, Worcester
Solo Artiste of the Year
Double H Country Music Club, Devon
Solo Artiste of the Year

1984
Smokey Mountain C&W Club, Wythall, Birmingham
Solo Artiste of the Year
Aberdeen Country & Western Club
Best British Solo Artiste
Smokestack Country Music Club, Taunton, Somerset
Best Solo Artiste
Double H Country Music Club, Devon
Solo Artiste of the Year

1985

Smokey Mountain C&W Club, Wythall, Birmingham
Solo Artiste of the Year
Aberdeen Country & Western Club
Best British Solo Artiste
Double H Country Music Club, Devon
Solo Artiste of the Year

1986

Wales Country Music Awards (Wrexham Lager Awards)
Charity Award (Lazyacre CMC)
Double H Country Music Club, Devon
Solo Artiste of the Year
Smokey Mountain C&W Club, Wythall, Birmingham
Solo Artiste of the Year
Aberdeen Country & Western Club
Best British Solo Artiste
Oswestry Orthopaedic Hospital
Special Award on behalf of the patients

1987

Double H Country Music Club, Devon
Solo Artiste of the Year
Wales Country Music Awards (Wrexham Lager Awards)
Charity Award (Lazyacre CMC)
Nashville CMC, Exeter
Solo Artiste of the Year
Aberdeen Country & Western Club
Best British Solo Artiste

1988

Nashville CMC, Exeter
Solo Artiste of the Year
Wales Country Music Awards
Charity Award (Lazyacre CMC)
Fry's Country Music Club, Keynsham, Bristol
Regular Outstanding Performance Award
Wales and Border Counties Festival Awards
Club Award (Lazyacre CMC)

1994
MEB "Heart of Britain" Awards
Tony Best
in recognition of his contribution to
improve the quality of life for others.

1995
Lazyacre Country Music Club
Most Popular Show (The Tony Best Laughter Show)

1997
Country Music News and Routes Newspaper
Achievement Award
Independent Promoter
Tony Best of Tony Best Leisure

1998
The Marc Wayne Memorial Award
Jean & Tony Best

2007
Inducted into
The British Country Music Hall of Fame

CHAPTER 38

Thanks

Firstly my thanks must go to my wife Jean and our daughter Lynne, both of whom wholeheartedly supported me in my decision to spend time putting on paper the stories of my life. They always knew that I had it in mind to do it someday, but they respected the fact that I felt I needed to wait until I had retired, enabling me to devote all my time to the project.

When I had finished writing the book I asked Lynne to take over the arrangements for the publication and printing of the book, and she has done a remarkable job.

Whilst I was actually writing the book each time I had completed a chapter I would take the pages to Jean and she would listen intently as I read out loud the newly written chapter. This gave us the chance to put right anything which was not quite correct as well as to enjoy recalling many of our wonderful times together. It was sort of proof reading by proxy and an enjoyable experience for both of us.

The reading out loud was also good for me because since my stroke my speech has not completely recovered. My speech therapist advised me that reading out loud is an excellent exercise for helping to restore my speech to normal. I have been very lucky with my recovery from the stroke, so if reading out loud helps then I am going to read out loud!

So both Jean and Lynne were very important in the writing and publication of the book, and they deserve my sincere thanks.

Punctuation, spelling and grammar have always been important to me, and obviously are most important in a project like this. So I asked a few close friends to help me by proofreading the copy and to point out any errors. They all did this most thoroughly and with great enthusiasm. A big thank you to John and Val Malam who diligently went through every page looking for any necessary corrections but also massaged my ego by telling me that they thought I had a best seller on my hands!

My second proofreaders were Phil and Josie Summers, who also scoured the book for errors and also offered very useful suggestions as to the lay out of some chapters. As I knew they would be Phil and Josie were exceptionally thorough and were a great help to me. Many, many thanks to you both.

After this I approached a close family friend, Angie Treherne. Many years ago back in the 1980s Angie's Mum and Dad, Eddie and Jessie Treherne were staunch members of Lazyacre, and very strong supporters, attending every show and coming with us on club holidays etc. Some years ago we lost both Eddie and Jessie when they passed away, but just by chance, three or four years ago, Lynne met up with Angie and the two of them hit it off right away. Since then they have become firm friends, and Jean and I have adopted her as a sort of second daughter. Angie read through the book for her adopted second Dad, and added her input to that of my other proofreaders. Thanks so much Angie.

Finally I must say a massive thank-you to Steve and his team at YouCaxton, my publishers, for their help and guidance in steering us through the publishing process. Their help has been invaluable.

CHAPTER 39

An Interesting Exercise

Dear Reader,

I have found it very strange! I have devoted all my time in the last few months putting these few words down on paper, hopefully for your interest, and much more hopefully, for your enjoyment.

It has certainly been a very interesting exercise for Jean and me. You will have seen that I have had a very varied life, whether it has been the full eighty years as Tony Jarrett, or just the last forty of them as Tony Best. Each page I have written about my life, I have lived again in my mind as I have put the words down on the page. Then Jean and I have relived them again as I read each completed page out loud to her, and together, we have once again, enjoyed the memorable incidents and experiences.

Of course, Jean wasn't with me for the first twenty years of my life, so very many of my recollections of my childhood and my teenage years at home and early days in the RAF were all new to her, and they were, she tells me, very interesting for her.

It has been tremendously enjoyable as I have brought back to mind and written about my times in the Royal Air Force, my life looking after a club and then a pub, a shop and an agency, before devoting the rest of my life to music, and the spin offs from my musical career like the leisure business. I have been blessed to have such a diverse life, and it has been nothing but a pleasure.

My original reason for writing these memoirs, was just to pass on a little insight into my life for my lovely grandchildren and great grandchildren. It was my wife, Jean and daughter, Lynne, who said to me, "You really must publish it, as there are many people who will find it of interest, not just family, but friends, club members, artistes, friends from our years in Anglesey and from your time in the music business. Then there are people from all over the country, who know you from having been on our holiday events, or seen you performing on stage, who would surely find it of interest." So that made my mind up for me and here it is.

Since the word got round that I was doing this, I have been amazed at the number of people who have shown an interest.

If you have enjoyed reading it, that pleases me very much. If not, then I hope at least I have kept it short enough not to have wasted too much of your precious time! At least I've loved doing it, and giving myself the chance to relive an enjoyable life all over again.

Where do I go from here?

Well, to be honest, I just don't know. I am now fully retired, and it is all very new to me. Never before have I looked into my diary and found blank pages with no gigs booked, or events or meetings or anything. I see there are a few hospital appointments and my fortnightly clubnights, but nothing else.

It's completely different to anything I've ever experienced before, this retirement business. I want to and I certainly intend to enjoy my retirement. Jean and I will definitely still want to take our trips to London to see some West End shows, and we look forward to our visits to the theatre nearer to home, so that is still on the cards. Also, we hope to make good use of our railcard to visit some of the friends we made on our travels in other parts of the country.

So what do you do when you're retired? I remember asking Ken Dodd if he was ever going to retire and he said to me, "I can't Tony, the only thing I can do is to stand on a stage and make people laugh. I don't have any hobbies or other interests, so I just carry on!" That's a bit like how I feel myself. I don't do any gardening, cooking, walking, going to the pub or socialising. My only hobby is the country music club, and I'm very lucky that this keeps me pretty busy, arranging the club programme and organising special events for the club members like trips out and other activities. It will be very interesting to see what I find to do with the rest of all this spare time I'm supposedly going to have.

I've had a very enjoyable first few months of my retirement, putting this book together. It has been a labour of love and has brought back to me and my family many happy memories, but once this goes to the publisher, what then? I just don't know at the moment.

However, I've never planned any part of my life in advance before so I don't suppose I'm going to start now! I'm confident something will turn up to keep me occupied. It always has in the past! I've heard so many people who have been retired for a while, and who say, "I'm so busy in my retirement, I just don't know how I found time to go to work!" Who knows? You might hear me saying that in a few months time.

Wish me luck!

Tony

THE FAMILY

The Best family and a few close friends

The Family - L to R - Lynne, Jackie, Tony, Gina, Beverley,
Jean, Thomas, Me,
Front - Zara and Adelaide (great grandaughters)

Left to right - Lynne, Michelle, Beverley, Jean

Paul and Michelle

Lynne with her son, Thomas and his wife, Gina

Michelle and Paul with the twins, Ernie and Hector

A happy "Nanna" with Edith, the twins' older sister

Ernie and Hector

Great Grandad Tony and Great Nanna Jean